LEINSTER
CONQUERING EUROPE

Peter Breen with the Leinster Team **Photographs by Inpho Photography**

LEINSTER
CONQUERING EUROPE

PENGUIN

IRELAND

PENGUIN IRELAND

Published by the Penguin Group
Penguin Ireland, 25 St Stephen's Green, Dublin 2, Ireland
(a division of Penguin Books Ltd)

Penguin Books Ltd, 80 Strand, London WC2R 0RL, England
Penguin Group (USA) Inc., 375 Hudson Street, New York,
New York 10014, USA

Penguin Group (Australia), 250 Camberwell Road,
Camberwell, Victoria 3124, Australia (a division of Pearson
Australia Group Pty Ltd)

Penguin Group (Canada), 90 Eglinton Avenue East, Suite 700,
Toronto, Ontario, Canada M4P 2Y3 (a division of Pearson Penguin
Canada Inc.)

Penguin Books India Pvt Ltd, 11 Community Centre,
Panchsheel Park, New Delhi – 110 017, India

Penguin Group (NZ), 67 Apollo Drive, Rosedale, North Shore 0632,
New Zealand (a division of Pearson New Zealand Ltd)

Penguin Books (South Africa) (Pty) Ltd, 24 Sturdee Avenue,
Rosebank, Johannesburg 2196, South Africa

Penguin Books Ltd, Registered Offices: 80 Strand, London
WC2R 0RL, England

www.penguin.com

First published 2009
1

Text copyright © Leinster Rugby, 2009
Photographs copyright © Inpho Photography, except for the
photographs on pages 124 and 125, copyright © David Cahill

The moral right of the author has been asserted

Set in Caecilia and Helvetica Neue
Designed by Smith & Gilmour, London
Printed and bound by Firmengruppe APPL, aprinta druck,
Wemding, Germany

A CIP catalogue record for this book is available from the
British Library

ISBN: 978-1-844-88222-9

www.greenpenguin.co.uk

Penguin Books is committed to a sustainable
future for our business, our readers and our planet.
The book in your hands is made from paper
certified by the Forest Stewardship Council.

FSC
Mixed Sources
Product group from well-managed
forests and other controlled sources
www.fsc.org Cert no. SA-COC-1592
© 1996 Forest Stewardship Council

CONTENTS

THE CAPTAIN

" A good leader inspires people to have confidence in the leader; a great leader inspires people to have confidence in themselves … **"**

(Anonymous)

SATURDAY, 2 MAY 2009, 7.45 P.M., CROKE PARK, HOME-TEAM DRESSING-ROOM

JOY There's no other word for what I'm feeling right now. The fear of losing drives you on in the build-up to games, but the delight in victory from days like this one is hard to describe.

PAIN You might have heard of a colleague of mine, a big fat Cook Islander (although not as fat as when I first saw him) by the name of Stan Wright. Certainly after the last two games – Harlequins three weeks ago and Munster today – Rocky Elsom and I have. I'm lying on a bench adjacent to the showers getting treatment after a clash of heads. It was the closing minutes and Niall Ronan took a quick tap, I tackled low but Stan came around the corner and smashed him, catching me on the way round. Something similar happened to Rocky during the 'Quins game when Stan accidentally busted his nose. Stan is one of our most consistent performers, someone who always plays with great heart and power. When I clashed with Stan all I remember was him going, 'Faack!' and then thinking, 'Oh my God, I think I might be blind.' I heard our doctor Arthur Tanner and physio

LEFT: Leo Cullen at the Heineken Cup launch

James Allen talking to me and when I came to, the ref was over looking to get the game started. He just said there was less than a minute left so I knew we were going to win. I ended up leaving the field with ice on my face and sat down on the icebox. I will laugh about the incident later, but the adrenalin has worn off and now all I can feel is pain. Pain, relief and satisfaction. I guess it's a small price to pay.

CONTROVERSY One of the more bizarre injuries I've had, but it seems bruising has seeped down into my eyes, making visibility difficult. Straight away there is a realization that we still have a final to play. Celebrations can be put on hold for another day. The final whistle blew shortly after I went off and I got up to clap the Munster players in and it was at this point that Alan Quinlan came over to me to apologize for an incident in the game. I remember doing a television interview with Drico and handing him the Man of the Match award. The Sky commentator asked me to remark on an earlier incident involving a Munster player – at that stage I didn't know who it was – when a hand came across and caught my eye while I was at the bottom of a ruck. At that point there was no question of gouging in my mind. It's something that happens in the heat of the moment. All I prefer to say to Sky is that Quinny is a guy who plays the game on the edge and someone whom I rate highly as a player and as a bloke. I've spoken to him and there's no issue between us. One of the aspects of this sport is that whatever happens on the pitch stays there. We return to the dressing-room and I can see the wounds of war on my face. I shower, change and next it's the second and third round of interviews with the Sunday and Monday media. It's the final and we're in new territory as a club now, soon to face either Cardiff Blues or Leicester. But there's a storm brewing. It's annoying because I'd rather people reflect on our performance than on one isolated, albeit unfortunate incident …

SUNDAY, 3 MAY 2009, 5.27 P.M., LIVING-ROOM AT HOME

FATE Well, it had to be Leicester, didn't it?

RIGHT: Cullen reaches for a lineout ball in the semi-final against Munster

CHAPTER 1
BOGEY SIDES

" One of our unwritten rules this year was that we would back up everything. **"**

A cruel autumn wind crashed against the marina in Malahide, Co. Dublin, as Leo Cullen and Michael Cheika arrived. The duo could have been forgiven for contracting 'Blue Flu' considering the events of the night before. They hardly had time to digest the 18–0 Magners League defeat to Munster before being whisked away to outline their European goals to an expectant audience at the launch of the 2008/9 Heineken Cup.

For Cullen, recently installed as Leinster captain, it was a chance to begin a new chapter. 'Events like the Irish launch of the Heineken Cup can take a couple of different angles. Obviously there's a lot of talk about the group you're in, your upcoming opponents and there's also attention on your most recent game to assess your form.

'For Leinster, this meant the night before when we lost to Munster in the RDS. Not what you'd call a fun night at the office.'

And the first people the duo met? 'Munster skipper Paul O'Connell and their new coach Tony McGahan!'

Cullen recalls: 'There was a lot of hype and an air of invincibility about Munster coming into the tournament, as they were reigning champions and a side who were flying in the early rounds of the league.'

LEFT: Brian O'Driscoll skips away from an Edinburgh tackler on the Murrayfield pitch where Leinster's European campaign began – and where they hoped it would conclude

ABOVE: Ulster captain Rory Best, Munster captain Paul O'Connell and Leinster captain Leo Cullen at the Irish launch of the Heineken Cup competition in Malahide, Co. Dublin

Back in June, Leinster had been drawn with their perennial nemesis Edinburgh; Castres Olympique, an unknown French quantity coached by Irishmen Mark McCall and Jeremy Davidson; and London Wasps, two-time winners of the competition.

Bernard Jackman had spent the summer months savouring Leinster's triumph in the previous season's Magners League, perhaps the greatest accomplishment in a career that had stretched over a decade. At this stage in his career, time was not an ally. 'One of our unwritten rules this year was that we would back up everything,' he says. 'If something was said, you did it. No excuses …'

The journey was under way.

The summer of 2008 had been a period of transition for the Leinster team. Leo Cullen replaced Brian O'Driscoll as captain, and Shane Jennings and Chris Whitaker were installed as vice-captains. Playing reinforcements arrived in the shape of C.J. van der Linde, a South African World Cup-winning prop; the versatile back Isa Nacewa, John Fogarty from Connacht,

> **❝** It was time for a change that summer, to update our playing style. **❞**

Simon Keogh, returning home after a successful spell in London with Harlequins, and an Australian back-row forward by the name of Rocky Elsom.

With Kurt McQuilkin, the former Leinster captain, having already established a reputation as one of European rugby's foremost defensive coaches, Michael Cheika turned to the recently retired All Black Jono Gibbes to replace Mike Brewer as forwards coach, with his good friend and former Randwick mentor Alan Gaffney also returning to a province where he retained strong links.

Since arriving in the summer of 2005, Cheika had spearheaded a major transformation – not just of the playing personnel but of the entire culture of a team that had enjoyed sporadic rather than sustained success.

'It was time for a change that summer, to update our playing style, and I was pleased with the new personalities,' Cheika says. 'Alan has a very good track record in the game and having been involved with Leinster before you could sense he had a real desire to bring success to the club.

'We had originally sounded out Jono to join as a player, but having met him it was clear that he could bring a fresh dynamic and organizational skills, and would take our forward play to a new level.

'Kurt is a Leinster man through and through, and over the last few years he has gotten better and better in his role. He is also very thorough in how he prepares.

'So overall I felt we had a good mix of experience and closeness to the current game, as well as continuity from the previous coaching structure.'

First up for Leinster in the Heineken Cup was their bogey side, Edinburgh. Cheika recalls: 'We went into the opening Heineken Cup game on the back of two Magners League defeats, which was far from ideal, and Edinburgh are a team that we had experienced difficulties playing against in the past ...'

NEXT PAGE: Rocky Elsom breaks away for a long-range solo try – his first Heineken Cup score, and Leinster's first points of the campaign

Devin Toner, the young 6'10" lock, faced into his European debut at Murrayfield with hopes of initially surviving, finding his feet and then thriving. 'It was my Heineken Cup debut and to get a start was brilliant. I only found out three days before the game because Mal [O'Kelly] withdrew late through injury, so I suppose there was less time to get nervous in the build-up.'

A first-half four-try blitz, with the bonus point secured by Shane Horgan's finish in the 35th minute, gave Leinster the platform they were looking for.

For Brian O'Driscoll the opening round was about sending out a clear message. 'It was important for the team to make a statement of intent early on in the campaign and the bonus-point victory in Edinburgh got us off on the front foot. You always want to start strongly and our first-half display that day was excellent.'

Facing into his first trip to Edinburgh in a blue jersey, Rocky Elsom didn't carry the emotional baggage of past Murrayfield disappointments.

'Against Connacht we made only three or four line-breaks all night so there was a strong onus on the boys to up their game significantly. Against Edinburgh it was vital that we got off to a good start. There was a lot of talk about them being our bogey team but I always felt that in terms of comparisons between the two teams, we were that bit stronger.'

As Shane Horgan raced clear for try number four, memories came flooding back for him.

'That ground has special memories for me this year, but it hasn't always been like that! I've experienced games where you would have a loud, vocal and partisan Scottish support against you. There have also been times in club matches with Edinburgh when the home support are outnumbered by visiting Leinster supporters and that looked to be the same coming into this game.

" That ground has special memories for me this year, but it hasn't always been like that! "

LEFT: Michael Cheika

ABOVE: Shane Horgan scores the bonus-point-securing fourth try

'There was quite a long build-up and it was important for us to lay down a marker for the competition itself as well as for ourselves against a team who had a bit of a hoodoo over us. There was a lot of external pressure because it had been a long time since a Leinster team had lost three games on the bounce.

'That pressure was a positive, because it focused our minds, and playing in a new competition certainly spurred us on.'

Horgan's try ensured a bonus point in the group, just reward for a fine collective effort.

'Although I never really measure myself on tries scored, as a winger it's always satisfying to score them because you feel like you're doing your small part at the end of a move, or a number of phases, to help the team. One thing's for sure, though, the older you get the hungrier you become to get them.'

As Stephen Keogh, a member of Munster's inaugural Heineken Cup winning panel, observed, it was a 'start as you mean to go on' kind of performance.

'Winning so convincingly, in a stadium which had historically not been the kindest to us, set a benchmark for the season. You could detect a feeling of confidence coming from the players that day.'

Edinburgh 16, Leinster 27
Saturday, 11 October 2008

Murrayfield, 1.35 p.m.
Attendance: 5,372

EDINBURGH: 15: Chris Paterson, 14: Mark Robertson (John Houston, 51), 13: Hugo Southwell (David Blair, 77), 12: Nick De Luca, 11: Simon Webster, 10: Phil Godman, 9: Mike Blair, captain; 1: Allan Jacobsen, 2: Ross Ford, 3: Geoff Cross, 4: Matt Mustchin, 5: Craig Hamilton (Ben Gissing, 59), 6: Scott Newlands (Craig Hamilton, 72), 7: Alan MacDonald, 8: Allister Hogg

LEINSTER: 15: Girvan Dempsey, 14: Shane Horgan, 13: Luke Fitzgerald, 12: Brian O'Driscoll (Jonathan Sexton, 79), 11: Rob Kearney, 10: Felipe Contepomi, 9: Chris Whitaker (Chris Keane, 68); 1: Stan Wright (Cian Healy, 41), 2: Bernard Jackman (John Fogarty, 73), 3: C.J. van der Linde, 4: Leo Cullen, captain, 5: Devin Toner (Trevor Hogan, 65), 6: Rocky Elsom, 7: Shane Jennings, 8: Jamie Heaslip

REPLACEMENTS NOT USED: Stephen Keogh, Gary Brown

EDINBURGH SCORERS: Penalty try, C. Paterson (2 penalties, 1 conversion), P. Godman (1 penalty)

LEINSTER SCORERS: F. Contepomi (1 try, 2 conversions, 1 penalty), R. Elsom / B. O'Driscoll / S. Horgan (1 try each)

REFEREE: Rob Debney (England)

CHAPTER 2
THE LEADER OF THE PACK

Jono Gibbes joined Leinster as forwards coach in the summer of 2008, replacing fellow New Zealander Mike Brewer. Gibbes, an uncompromising back-row forward in his day, was capped on eight occasions for his country and featured in 68 Super-14 clashes for the Waikato Chiefs. He also captained the New Zealand Maori side to victory over the 2005 touring British and Irish Lions.

With the Experimental Law Variations coming into play in the northern hemisphere at the start of the 2008/9 season, it was felt that the practical experience garnered by Gibbes towards the latter end of his playing days in the southern hemisphere, where the modifications were already being trialled, would be beneficial for the team.

'It was a big move for me, in a sense a trip into the unknown,' he says. 'It was not only a new role, but it was a new country, a new competition against new teams, so at first it was a little bit daunting but I soon enough settled in.

'I was familiar with Leinster and coming into the set-up I knew that there was a core of experienced forwards in the pack, so it wasn't as if that area needed radical reconstruction.

'One thing that definitely struck me was that I became far more nervous around games, because you have no real control once the players cross the whitewash.

'I was a bit naive about the opening Heineken Cup win in Edinburgh. They had more or less the Scottish pack so between their club and international commitments they had played together a lot. It was only as the season unfolded that I really grasped the resonance of winning on the road in Europe. I felt that we had played well for 40 minutes but I was disappointed that we didn't continue in the second half. In reflection to get a five-point win away from home was a fantastic result and it laid the platform for us.'

❝ It was a big move for me, a trip into the unknown. ❞

CHAPTER 3
WHERE IS THY STING?

❝ We had to match them physically first and foremost and be at our best. They nearly play a Rugby League style of game against you. **❞**

Wasps came into the second round of group matches on the back of an unconvincing display at home to Castres. Leinster's first home game of the campaign, against the team perceived to be their strongest rivals in the group, was always going to be the acid test: winning at home in the group stages is paramount. In some quarters the match was being billed as an unofficial trial of sorts for the recently installed Lions coaching ticket, which featured Wasps coaches Ian McGeechan and Shaun Edwards.

'Wasps are one of the big four teams in Europe, alongside Munster, Leicester and Toulouse, who always save their best form for the Heineken Cup,' says Shane Jennings, 'so when we were drawn against them I think we were all cautious.

'Even though they had started the season poorly, I know from my two years with Leicester that they had the ability to turn it on. We had to match them physically first and foremost and be at our best. They nearly play a Rugby League style of game against you.'

For Devin Toner, who was thrust into the limelight for the second time in as many matches after skipper Leo Cullen suffered an injury early on, it was anxious times. 'It's hard when you're coming on as a sub, particularly

LEFT: Jamie Heaslip (left) and Luke Fitzgerald get stuck in to Wasps wing Paul Sackey

PREVIOUS PAGE: Brian
O'Driscoll reaches for
his first try of a brilliant
first half

when it's that early in a game and you're not expecting it.

'I really felt for Leo and there's a part of you that feels bad because you don't want to, in a way, profit from another's misfortune, but that's the name of the game,' Toner says. 'Coming up against Simon Shaw and Tom Palmer on my home debut in the competition was an eye opener, you could say …'

Two moments of magic in a peerless first-half display from Brian O'Driscoll gave the hosts a half-time advantage.

The Ireland captain recalls that confidence was high as Leinster welcomed the two-time champions to the RDS. 'Whenever you come up against an English team there's always that added edge,' he admitted. 'Wasps, like Leicester, are the standard-bearers historically in Europe so that was an important step in our campaign.

'The pack laid the platform and the backs capitalized on the chances. The first try was more opportunistic than anything and there was a great bit of skill on the touchline from Kearns, who nudged the ball with his right foot into my path and I gathered and fell over to score.

'For the second try, Whits saw that I was alongside him on the blind side. He sucked the last defender in brilliantly and I knew as Eoin Reddan came in I'd have to chip him and try to regather. The key was the ball going up and down quickly and I wouldn't say Jeremy [Staunton] covered himself in glory with his defensive effort when he came in to challenge me!'

O'Driscoll chipped to himself for a second time, his foot snatching the ball from between Staunton's hands.

'I was willing the ball to come down because Tom Voyce was closing in on me and thankfully I got over the whitewash, just. Though we conceded a try just before half-time we got better and better in the second half and it was an important stepping stone in the context of the group.'

> **❝ I was willing the ball to come down because Tom Voyce was closing in on me and thankfully I got over the whitewash, just. ❞**

Unfortunately, O'Driscoll tore knee ligaments and could not continue in the second half.

Felipe Contepomi, the scorer of 16 points, was instrumental in the rout and after his 56th-minute charge-down try he struck a 'Christ the Redeemer' pose as his team-mates basked in the glory of the second successive bonus point.

'I play rugby to enjoy it,' the Argentinian playmaker says. 'I come from a football-orientated culture and I was never one for individual sports like golf or tennis. Whenever I scored a try I never planned the celebration. You just do what's natural, what's instinctive in sharing that moment with your team-mates and in no way looking to disrespect your opponents. It's a South American thing, nothing more.

'Coming into the Wasps game it was crucial that we put them under pressure early on because they had started poorly in their league and we were coming off the back of that fantastic win in Edinburgh. They were the big team for us to beat.'

ABOVE: Felipe Contepomi's try was the highlight of a 16-point effort from the out-half

For Malcolm O'Kelly it was another big step on the journey. For the first time, he believed, the big clubs across Europe sat up and took notice. 'This was an unbelievable win and it put us on the map.

'To live up to the standard of our second-half performance was always going to be difficult, but the important part about our approach this year was that we had the maturity to know that it didn't mean we'd win automatically.'

The November internationals provided a chance for Leinster to plot the downfall of Castres in the home-and-away fixtures before Christmas. But things didn't go quite to plan …

Leinster 41, Wasps 11
Saturday, 18 October 2008

RDS, 5.30 p.m.
Attendance: 18,300

LEINSTER: 15: Girvan Dempsey, 14: Shane Horgan, 13: Brian O'Driscoll (Jonathan Sexton, 41), 12: Luke Fitzgerald (Gary Brown, 68), 11: Rob Kearney, 10: Felipe Contepomi, 9: Chris Whitaker (Chris Keane, 74); 1: Stan Wright, 2: Bernard Jackman (John Fogarty, 74), 3: C. J. van der Linde, 4: Leo Cullen, captain (Devin Toner, 14), 5: Malcolm O'Kelly (Stephen Keogh, 73), 6: Rocky Elsom, 7: Shane Jennings, 8: Jamie Heaslip

WASPS: 15: Jeremy Staunton (Mark van Gisbergen, 68), 14: Paul Sackey, 13: Josh Lewsey, 12: Riki Flutey, 11: Tom Voyce, 10: Danny Cipriani, 9: Eoin Reddan (Mark Robinson, 68); 1: Tim Payne (Pat Barnard, 69), 2: Rafael Ibanez, captain (Rob Webber, 53), 3: Phil Vickery, 4: Simon Shaw, 5: Tom Palmer, 6: James Haskell, 7: Tom Rees (Serge Betsen, 72), 8: Joe Worsley

LEINSTER SCORERS: B. O'Driscoll (2 tries), F. Contepomi (1 try, 4 conversions, 1 penalty), L. Fitzgerald / R. Elsom / Kearney (1 try each)

WASPS SCORERS: J. Staunton (1 try), D. Cipriani (2 penalties)

REFEREE: Nigel Owens (Wales)

RIGHT: Jonathan Sexton, who replaced the injured Brian O'Driscoll at half-time, played his part as Leinster ran away with the match in the second half

BACK TO THE FUTURE

You wake up one morning and life throws you a curveball.

The year was 1983. For seven years Alan Gaffney had been concentrating on raising a young family with his wife Lorraine in Sydney and in furthering his professional business career in commercial industrial real estate. When he retired from rugby in 1976 he had no real aspiration to come back as a coach, but he harboured a hope that he might one day see his son and daughter establish a playing or administrative affiliation with the world-renowned Randwick club – the 'Galloping Greens' – where he had built many enduring friendships.

Then he received a call from Randwick (and later Wallaby) head coach Bob Dwyer, who asked if he wanted to get involved.

'Bob Dwyer was years ahead of his time,' Gaffney says. 'He revolutionized attack and he devised a system that got the best out of what was an outstanding generation of players in Randwick. When he first enquired about me joining him I was a bit surprised because I had been out of the game for so long, but I agreed and coached the senior team in year one, the Colts [youth teams] for the next two years and back with the senior team for the remainder of the subsequent fourteen years in amateur rugby.

Gaffney would go on to enjoy spells with the New South Wales under-21s team as an assistant coach in the burgeoning Waratahs franchise (1997–9) before beginning a love affair with Ireland.

A talented and uncompromising number 8, Cheika, the son of a Lebanese immigrant, joined Randwick as a seventeen-year-old one year into Gaffney's first term as a Randwick coach. It was to be the start of a lasting friendship.

'We both came from Rugby League backgrounds and we got on almost immediately. In 1986 he would have gone into the senior ranks and joined players like Simon Poidevin, Mick Murray and Tony Daly, David Knox, Timmy Kava, Lloyd Walker, Warwick Waugh, David Campese and a host of other Australian internationals.'

Gaffney's first two-year spell with Leinster under Matt Williams coincided with success for the team as they lifted the inaugural Celtic League title, and he carried the attacking ethos he honed with him to Munster, Australia and then Saracens. Then, one day, another phone call: Michael Cheika, now head coach at Leinster, wanted him to come back aboard.

CHAPTER 5
THREE FROM THREE

Leinster went into the November international break sitting pretty at the top of the pool, but the injury count was starting to mount. Isa Nacewa, still nursing a broken arm that had caused him to miss the first two Heineken Cup matches, was joined on the sidelines for the Castres home tie by Contepomi, Cullen and Jennings. The depth of the squad would be put to the test.

Nacewa, frustrated by the delay in making his European bow, was given a short break during the November international series. 'I was well on the road to recovery after my arm break against the Ospreys, so with the break for the November internationals I was given a bit of time off to attend my brother Ilaisa's wedding back in Australia. My sister Dot lives in London so it was nice for my fiancée and me to visit her.

'We also made a short trip to Edinburgh. I was hoping that it wouldn't be my last visit to the Scottish capital for the year.'

Contepomi missed out on an appearance in Croke Park for Argentina because of a hand infection. 'That was hard for me because since moving to Ireland it was always an ambition to play in that stadium. At this stage I was hoping to get back into action before Christmas, but the odds were against me making the Castres game in France.'

LEFT: Bernard Jackman, sporting a not-entirely-secure bandage over a head wound, scores his first-ever Heineken Cup try

ABOVE: Chris Whitaker
produces quick ball
off a ruck

Leo Cullen notes that 'The psychology behind playing sides back-to-back can be more difficult than when there's a few months separating games between two teams in a pool. The most famous case of score reversals was when Toulouse put 100 points on Ebbw Vale at home and then lost away the following week. I had some similar experience myself from a game against Stade Français ten years ago when we lost heavily in Paris [39–6] but won the return leg in Donnybrook.

'We came into the home match with 10 points out of 10 so people perhaps got carried away with the assumption that we were going to get two easy wins.'

'Expectations had risen that we'd score four tries again,' Shane Horgan recalls, 'but that was easier said than done. Castres were unlike any other French team we'd played in recent years because they had that bit of insider knowledge in Mark McCall and Jeremy Davidson, who were their coaches. I had come across both at various Ireland training sessions in my earlier days and had played with Jeremy a few times for Ireland, and Mark knew

" Castres were unlike any other French team we'd played in recent years because they had that bit of insider knowledge in Mark McCall and Jeremy Davidson. "

our individual and collective styles from his stint with Ulster. That insight certainly helped them.'

For recently graduated Academy flanker Sean O'Brien, making his European debut in the absence of Shane Jennings was a huge step, but he was determined not to change. 'The thing I've learned whenever you get good news about selection is to keep cool, not do anything different and go about your business as usual,' O'Brien says.

'When the team was picked in the middle of the week my first reaction was, "Oh God, what's happening here!" It was an incredible feeling, going from watching Heineken Cup games a year before to now being involved in them. I was level-headed enough to know that I had to perform.

'The earlier kick-off didn't affect me so much because I'd be an early riser. My father Sean is a builder back in Tullow, and a part-time cattle farmer, so there was always work to be done at home.

'Over the course of the season a lot of the senior players had good words of advice, and I suppose Birch's [Bernard Jackman's] point – "keep doing what you've been doing all along" – is something I've really tried to stick by. I like to get down to the ground and stay quite relaxed on match days, just chatting to the lads or having a walk on the pitch. Then when Cheiks gives his final team-talk it's time to switch on.

'Because French clubs can travel poorly in European competitions and we were coming off the back of two straight bonus-point wins, there was a perception that the game would be a walkover. Perhaps we were guilty of not taking our chances, but we knew that we weren't going to get things easy. I enjoyed the game. The atmosphere was good and the game was physical and high tempo.'

ABOVE: Brian O'Driscoll
scores Leinster's
second try, which
was converted for
a 26–3 lead

Bernard Jackman suffered an early cut to his head – but it didn't do him any harm, as he went on to score his first European try since a Challenge Cup effort for the Sale in 2001/2.

'I like to shave my head the day before every game and at this stage of my career it has become a part of my pre-match routine,' he says. 'I don't know whether the skin on the top of my head is particularly soft or more prone to cuts, but I took a bang on it which needed staples early on in the first half. I put on a head guard to protect the bandage and went back out to play.

'I don't usually wear a head guard and it didn't feel comfortable so at some stage I'd had enough and I threw it on the sidelines. In one of the subsequent scrums the bandage became loose and when I came back after the second it was flapping off my head like a sail in the wind. But it might have been a good omen because I managed to get on the score-sheet for my first Heineken Cup try …'

The evergreen Kiwi out-half David Holwell, who had joined on a short-term deal to cover Contepomi's injury, was a second-half substitute for Jonathan

Sexton, whose growing reputation was enhanced by 14 points. Holwell capped a wonderful cameo with a drop-kick conversion from the touchline after Simon Keogh's 76th-minute try as Leinster chased a third straight bonus point. But there wasn't to be a fourth try.

With Cullen still absent, Devin Toner earned the Man of the Match honour for a (literally) towering display.

'There are benefits and disadvantages to being 6'10",' he explained. 'When you mess up there's nowhere to hide, but when you can get dominance in lineouts, which extends the size of your body even more, then there are rewards.'

Doing the Man of the Match interview for television was a new experience: 'Although I have done a bit of media days and interviews over the last few years, I was a bit nervous because it's Sky and you become conscious that what you say is going to nearly every rugby club, pub and sporting household across Europe and even beyond. I'd like to think I have a pretty good head, and although I'm not shy, I would be quiet and tend to

ABOVE: Simon Keogh dives for the final score of the afternoon

keep my concentration on just answering the question.

'A lot of the questions in the post-match press conference centred on us not getting a bonus point and the challenge that we would face in France the following week. Me, I was just happy that the team were winning and we were picking up important points. To be getting games at the highest level and picking up bits of experience as I went along was a massive bonus.'

Knowing the European landscape at this time of year, and looking forward to the arduous prospect of a trip to France, Girvan Dempsey was not expecting a capitulation.

❝I was just happy that the team were winning and we were picking up important points. ❞

'Having buried the ghosts of Murrayfield and come out of the Wasps game at home with bonus points, we had laid down a marker, but the Castres home match was tough.

'In the build-up to the away game people said that a win in France in the return leg would tee us up nicely for qualification, but that thought didn't enter our heads at the time. We knew how difficult any trip to France could be …'

Leinster 33, Castres Olympique 3
Saturday, 6 December 2008

RDS, 1.35 p.m.
Attendance: 16,500

LEINSTER: 15: Girvan Dempsey (Simon Keogh, 71), 14: Shane Horgan, 13: Brian O'Driscoll (Brian Blaney, 72), 12: Luke Fitzgerald, 11: Rob Kearney, 10: Jonathan Sexton (David Holwell, 61), 9: Chris Whitaker, captain (Chris Keane, 67); 1: Stan Wright (C. J. van der Linde, 76), 2: Bernard Jackman, 3: C. J. van der Linde (Cian Healy, 68), 4: Devin Toner (Trevor Hogan, 68), 5: Malcolm O'Kelly, 6: Rocky Elsom, 7: Sean O'Brien (Stephen Keogh, 71), 8: Jamie Heaslip

CASTRES: 15: Cameron McIntyre, 14: Charles Sika, 13: Steve Kefu, 12: Lionel Mazars, 11: Rafael Carbello (Thomas Bouquié, 15), 10: Anthony Lagardère, 9: Kevin Senio; 1: Gideon Lensing (Yannick Forestier, 50), 2: Mathiou Bonollo (Akvsenti Giorgadze, 55), 3: Luc Ducalcon (Fabio Staibano, 57), 4: Ludovic Michaux (Joe Tekori, 70), 5: Colin Gaston, captain, 6: Lei Tomiki, 7: Darron Nell (Steve Malonga, 27), 8: Florian Faure

LEINSTER SCORERS: B. Jackman / B. O'Driscoll / Sim. Keogh (1 try each), J. Sexton (1 conversion, 4 penalties), D. Holwell (2 conversions)

CASTRES SCORERS: A. Lagardère (1 penalty)

REFEREE: Peter Allan (SRU)

CHAPTER 6

THE MINISTER OF DEFENCE

In nine Heineken Cup matches, Leinster conceded a meagre tally of five tries, one of which was a penalty try. It is an impressive record, which the team – and defence coach Kurt McQuilkin – are proud of.

A former Leinster captain who made fifteen Heineken Cup appearances for the province and won five Ireland caps, McQuilkin rejoined the province as defence coach after coaching stints with Ireland at under-19, under-21 and Sevens levels. 'Coming back into the Leinster set-up after being away for the last few years was like coming back to a completely new club,' says McQuilkin. 'The facilities, infrastructure, personnel had all changed immeasurably and it was a far cry from the old days.

'At first I was a bit anxious as to how the players, some of whom I would have played with, would react, but their professionalism shone through from day one. Even the feel around matches is different for me now. Once the captain's run is over my work is effectively done until the warm-up. As I've gotten older the one thing you realize is that nothing beats playing.'

McQuilkin says 'teams are getting smarter' defensively, but it's a constant struggle to stay ahead. 'The important thing to remember is that as sides' defences are improving, so are teams' attacking prowess, and that's something that I don't want to see! Seriously, though, there's lots of good aggressive defensive play that is the foundation of a lot of sides' offence.'

External criticism of Leinster for past Heineken Cup failures did not go unnoticed, McQuilkin says. 'You take criticism of the team personally because it affects you. You'd be lying if you said that it doesn't. You can lie down or be galvanized, and that drive came from within the squad, not to prove the doubters wrong but to become more ruthless in everything we did.'

❝ You take criticism of the team personally. ❞

CHAPTER 7
THE NIGHTMARE BEFORE CHRISTMAS

Freezing temperatures greeted the squad in Toulouse-Blagnac Airport, where an Arctic chill wreaked havoc on supporters planning to visit the balmy South of France.

For Isa Nacewa, returning to the side from injury, the visit to Castres was a trip into the unknown. 'When you have missed out on any length of rugby, as I had, you just want to get back playing. I wasn't signed by Leinster to sit on the sidelines and my early taste of Magners League action had whetted my appetite to play on the biggest stages.

'That Friday in December was strange. I was obviously delighted to be back playing and it was going to be a new experience for me to play in France. But as soon as we arrived on the Thursday afternoon the weather cut you like a knife. It was absolutely freezing.

'Ask any player and he will probably tell you that the best slots to play in are early afternoon, but when you have to kill time for a 9 p.m. kick-off in a foreign country, where the only TV channel at your disposal is the BBC World Service, and it's far too cold to have a walk around outside, you just adapt. It was certainly a new experience, though!'

For Malcolm O'Kelly, who had visited the likes of Bourgoin, Agen, Biarritz,

ABOVE: Castres defenders have Rocky Elsom in their sights

Toulouse and Stade Français over his long Leinster career, it was a new opponent but a familiar potential peril.

'When we played in France, back in the day, it was like a busman's holiday,' he says. 'You'd fly to Paris and then get the slow train down south. The whole trip would take over fourteen hours and you'd be exhausted. Different times.'

Girvan Dempsey recalls a bitter evening of extremities, on and off the field. 'You walk out of the hotel and it's freezing, you get off the coach and walk into the stadium and it's the same. Then when you walk on to the pitch before the warm-up you instinctively start running around because of the cold.

'Their winger, Charles Sika, ran on to the field with leggings on just as the game was going to kick off! That held up the action for a few minutes as the match officials instructed him to remove them.

Jonathan Sexton started the game strongly with a try and a difficult touchline conversion for Dempsey's try as the visitors turned the screw

early on, but collective missed opportunities in the Stade Pierre-Antoine cost the team dearly.

ABOVE: One bright spot for Leinster was the return from injury of Isa Nacewa, who came on as a second-half sub

'Indiscipline, ultimately, cost us,' Dempsey says. 'We conceded far too many penalties and, although we managed to get two tries, from myself and Sexto, we didn't trust in our defensive system.'

Rocky Elsom cited issues with the side's attack as a major contributing factor in the second-half slump. 'In the RDS a week previously we had dominated their lineout, but they threw us off guard with their approach that night.'

Felipe Contepomi agrees that indiscipline cost the team a victory, which could have all but wrapped up the top spot in the group. The result left the door wide open for Wasps to strike.

'Playing in France doesn't require a different mindset, but you must be two things – strong in defence and disciplined.

'This game was a crucial part of our season. We performed poorly, without a doubt, but the way that it was written suggested that we had

ABOVE: Chris Whitaker and Devin Toner trudge off after a narrow defeat

no backbone, no integrity and that level of criticism hurt ourselves, but especially our families.

At half-time, Contepomi, who had recovered from the injury that kept him out of the first Castres match, came on for Sexton at out-half. 'You can't argue when someone like Felipe comes on because he's a world-class player,' Sexton says. 'I was happy to score the try, but I missed some kicks that I really should have got.

'There are reasons why things don't go right. I hate making excuses because if you're declared fit then you have to get on with it, but I was dying with the flu for a fortnight beforehand. The pitch was also a bog to play on.

'Still, deep down it was a game I should have done better in and it was the lowest point of the season for me. It can either break you or strengthen your resolve and I wasn't going to give up. I spoke to Cheiks and I understood where he was coming from so I was determined to come back strongly.'

If it wasn't for bad luck, prop Ronan McCormack – who was in the 22-man squad for a European match for the first time in his career – would have had no luck at all. 'I had waited two years on the sidelines to be involved in a Heineken Cup 22,' he says, 'but after we lost this game I thought I must be an unlucky charm.'

The lateness of the kick-off meant that supporters and team alike stayed the night in the picturesque 'fortified place', to use the literal and somewhat apt interpretation of the town's Latin name of Castrum, before travelling home from Toulouse-Blagnac Airport the following morning.

The team went into the Christmas period knocked but not down. The coming weeks would be a test not only of their skills but also their character.

Castres Olympique 18, Leinster 15
Friday, 12 December 2008

Stade Pierre-Antoine, 9 p.m.
Attendance: 6,788

CASTRES: 15: Thomas Bouquié, 14: Charles Sika, 13: Steve Kefu, 12: Lionel Mazars, 11: Philip Christophers, 10: Anthony Lagardère (Kevin Senio, 80), 9: Sébastien Tillous-Borde; 1: Gideon Lensing, 2: Akvsenti Giorgadze (Mathieu Bonello, 77), 3: Daniel Strydom Saayman (Luc Ducalcon, 48), 4: Joe Tekori (Kirill Kulemin, 74), 5: Lionel Nallet, captain, 6: Lei Tomiki, 7: Chris Masoe, 8: Florian Faure

LEINSTER: 15: Girvan Dempsey, 14: Simon Keogh (Isa Nacewa, 67), 13: Brian O'Driscoll, 12: Luke Fitzgerald, 11: Rob Kearney, 10: Jonathan Sexton (Felipe Contepomi, 41), 9: Chris Whitaker, captain; 1: Cian Healy, 2: Bernard Jackman (Brian Blaney, 71), 3: Stan Wright, 4: Devin Toner, 5: Malcolm O'Kelly, 6: Rocky Elsom, 7: Shane Jennings, 8: Jamie Heaslip

REPLACEMENTS NOT USED: Ronan McCormack, Trevor Hogan, Sean O'Brien, Chris Keane

CASTRES SCORERS: A. Lagardère (6 penalties)

LEINSTER SCORERS: J. Sexton (1 try, 1 conversion), G. Dempsey (1 try), F. Contepomi (1 penalty)

REFEREE: David Pearson (England)

CHAPTER 8
AMERICAN DREAMS

In a tiny pocket of south-west Florida on the morning of 23 May, Victor Costello sat alone in his living-room. The idyllic Marco Island is the largest of the state's Ten Thousand Islands, located on the Gulf of Mexico. It has never been much of a rugby stronghold.

Gathering his thoughts ahead of the final, which kicked off at midday local time, and which he'd be watching thanks to a live feed from Setanta via Sky Sports, Costello reflected on the wave of good fortune that had now washed across Ireland's eastern province.

He'd dreamed of days like this over a professional career spanning ten years. Heineken Cup finals were events for other teams – les Toulousains, Munster, Wasps and Leicester – European aristocrats one and all. He had come close, but had never played a final.

Since his retirement in 2005 he had continued his love affair with the province of his birth, sometimes in the studio or in the press box, but always with his heart on his sleeve. On the day of the Heineken Cup semi-final three weeks earlier he was conspicuous in a Leinster jersey in the Croke Park media centre. Old habits and all that.

Cruelly, a long-standing commitment to return to Florida coincided with the biggest day in Leinster's history, so he had to improvise. Make his home a fortress of its own. Turn Marco Island blue, but this time from within.

'It was hard being away from Edinburgh and it's doubly hard when you're on your own watching Leinster matches without someone to bounce ideas off. So I had a few friends around and we all sat down to watch the game.

'I was confident that this was Leinster's year, even coming into the Munster game when virtually everyone had written us off. The blend of youth and experience peaking at the right time was, for me, the key factor behind the win.

'It was a long season. The knives were out and some of the performances had kicked up a lot of dust, but they believed in themselves.

'Looking at Croke Park on May 2nd, the team and the Leinster support wiped the floor with Munster. We now have a team of high achievers who have managed to maintain success at schools, club and international levels. There's nothing you can say about a player that he doesn't already know. What I admired most about this year was the manner in which the team addressed the deficiencies as a group and sourced that strength from within.

'Whenever I watch Leinster nowadays I don't feel maudlin or sad, nor do I long for times past. The way I see it, playing for Leinster was an honour, not a right. When Drico mentioned myself and some of the past players in his interview on the pitch after the final it really hit me like a hammer. It was a complete surprise and a really emotional gesture for him to make. I can't help but think that maybe in the midst of the joy of that moment, he thought about all the hard yards that paved the path to glory.'

" The knives were out and some of the performances had kicked up a lot of dust, but they believed in themselves. **"**

RIGHT: Costello was capped 126 times for Leinster and 39 times for Ireland

CHAPTER 9
INTO THE WASPS' NEST

The team arrived home to Dublin Airport on a Saturday afternoon after the defeat at Castres. While the majority of the group made their way home, hooker Bernard Jackman made the short trip to the Santry Sports Clinic for knee surgery. The inner wounds, however, were harder to take.

'It was a horrible feeling waiting for the plane to depart that Saturday morning,' the veteran hooker says. 'The dressing-room was a sombre place in the aftermath of the game and the mood hardly changed.

'There were hundreds of supporters and you knew what they were thinking. You could only imagine their disappointment. During my recovery from surgery I made up my mind that I would do everything in my power to right that wrong.'

Having spent only one of the last nine Christmases back home in Buenos Aires, Felipe Contepomi, like most of the foreign players, knows how hard it can be to spend the holidays away from home. So he was delighted to extend a welcome to a recent recruit from abroad, to give him a sense of home.

'In my first few years with Leinster friends like Derek Hegarty and Denis Hickie invited me around to their homes to share in the celebrations with their families and that meant a lot to me,' Contepomi says. 'It's important

LEFT: Luke Fitzgerald leaves a Wasps tackler grabbing fresh air

ABOVE: Aussie Rocky Elsom, spending his first Christmas in Ireland, ate Christmas dinner at the home of transplanted Argentinian Felipe Contepomi

to make everyone feel welcome when they join from a new country, when players are without the support base of family, so Rocky was a welcome guest to our house on Christmas day. With the Magners League game against Ulster in Belfast on December 27th, there wasn't much time to go overboard.'

Gordon D'Arcy's comeback around the turn of the year was like a new signing to the panel, giving the backline another experienced dimension.

'It was very frustrating missing the first few months of the season, and the injury had carried over from the previous year, which was hard,' D'Arcy says. 'I spoke to Cheiks and once I knew that he was planning to play me in the Magners League game up in Belfast after Christmas, I could start really building towards the next month ahead.'

Successive Magners League victories over Ulster, Connacht and the Cardiff Blues helped restore Leinster's confidence coming into the top-of-the-table clash with Wasps. The match was played at Twickenham instead of Wasps' usual home venue of Adams Park to accommodate a wider support base, and over 33,000 spectators, including some 15,000 travelling fans, gathered in the home of English rugby, with Wasps still smarting from the 30-point drubbing inflicted in October.

For prop Stan Wright, it was a once-in-a-lifetime experience, pitting himself against a World Cup-winning prop. 'Playing in Twickenham was awesome. I always wanted to play there and I was buzzing just to get out. I started at loose-head that day and I was up against Phil Vickery. The bigger the name, the more it drives me. And it doesn't get much bigger than an England and Lions prop. I know that if I'm not on my game then that will have an effect on the team. As long as I get my job done and do my best then I'm happy.'

Unfortunately, Wright had to exit injured in the first half, as did C.J. van der Linde, meaning the rest of the match was played with uncontested scrums.

Girvan Dempsey says that the adverse attention in the build-up didn't detract from the team's focus, but the will to qualify, instead, was the primary motivating factor. 'A lot of the press had written us off, saying that there was no way out of the group. The old stereotypes of us being soft and having no heart resurfaced and it wasn't a nice time, but it made us more driven, not to prove our detractors wrong, but to prove to ourselves that we had the strength of mind from within to get us out of this hole.'

Leo Cullen recalls, 'Confidence wasn't sky high in the camp as we faced into Christmas. We were in the public eye after the backlash from the defeat in Castres and there was a Christmas nightout planned in Naas. I really believe that nightsout like this are valuable to boost team spirit and it also enables players to get issues off their chests in a relaxed atmosphere.'

Shortly after 6.45 p.m. D'Arcy began warming up on the sideline. He looked around Twickenham, a ground where he had previously enjoyed success with Ireland, and he knew that he was ready. His second-half appearance as a substitute was the latest step in his comeback, and a significant one at that.

'Fifty-five minutes in and I was stepping on to the field in Twickenham for my first Heineken Cup appearance of the season.

'Okay we lost the game, never an easy result to take, but the grit that we showed – particularly evident in Luke [Fitzgerald]'s try-saving tackle in the closing minutes when he dragged the Wasps attacker down with unbelievable upper body strength – was encouraging.'

ABOVE: Cian Healy, an early sub for the injured C.J. van der Linde, looks for a bit of space

Fitzgerald recalls: 'It was more a double tackle, with Brian also playing a key role. I got a few fingertips to Lewsey's collar and managed to take him down before he got to the line. Lucky for us we managed to turn it over and survive another onslaught. It was fitting that it was our defence that got us through the group stages and it was a sign of things to come.'

The tackle meant that Leinster lost by just seven points – enough to earn a bonus point.

'That bonus point was crucial in the context of our qualification,' D'Arcy says. 'And it was vital that we built on that confidence for a season-defining game in the RDS the following weekend.'

> **"** The old stereotypes of us being soft and having no heart resurfaced and it wasn't a nice time. **"**

Felipe Contepomi, the scorer of all 12 Leinster points that evening, was proud of the gutsy nature of the display. 'This was a game in which we fought to the last minute. We knew that we had to get something in Twickenham and the bravery we showed in the closing quarter indicated that we were moving in the right direction. Believe me, I was glad of the eight-day turnaround before the next game!'

It would be the biggest match of the season. Leinster's destiny remained in their own hands.

Wasps 19, Leinster 12
Saturday, 17 January 2009

Twickenham, 5.35 p.m.
Attendance: 33,282

WASPS: 15: Mark van Gisbergen, 14: Paul Sackey, 13: Dom Waldouck (Tom Voyce, 65), 12: Riki Flutey, 11: Josh Lewsey, 10: Danny Cipriani (David Walder, 69), 9: Eoin Reddan (Joseph Simpson, 79), 1: Tim Payne (Dan Leo, 64), 2: Rob Webber, 3: Phil Vickery, captain, 4: George Skivington, 5: Richard Birkett, 6: Joe Worsley, 7: Serge Betsen, 8: James Haskell

LEINSTER: 15: Rob Kearney, 14: Shane Horgan (Brian O'Driscoll, 61), 13: Brian O'Driscoll (Gordon D'Arcy, 57), 12: Felipe Contepomi, 11: Luke Fitzgerald, 10: Isa Nacewa (Girvan Dempsey, 79), 9: Chris Whitaker, 1: Stan Wright (Sean O'Brien, 37), 2: Bernard Jackman (John Fogarty, 73), 3: C.J. van der Linde (Cian Healy, 17), 4: Leo Cullen, captain (Trevor Hogan, 17), 5: Malcolm O'Kelly, 6: Rocky Elsom, 7: Shane Jennings, 8: Jamie Heaslip

REPLACEMENT NOT USED: Chris Keane

WASPS SCORERS: S. Betsen (1 try), D. Cipriani (3 penalties, 1 conversion), D. Walder (1 penalty)

LEINSTER SCORERS: F. Contepomi (4 penalties)

REFEREE: Christophe Berdos (France)

CHAPTER 10
THE MARATHON MAN

Denis Hickie, who retired from rugby after the 2007 World Cup, is perhaps the most talented and most decorated of the generation of Leinster players who fell just short of the finish line in the marathon that is the Heineken Cup. But he enjoyed watching the 2009 Leinster team make the breakthrough. 'The Harlequins game summed up the great strides the team made,' Hickie says. 'It was a turning point, coming, as it did, on the back of probably the worst fifteen-minute spell at the beginning of the game, when nothing seemed to be going right. It took a lot of guts to hang on in there and the benefits for the remaining two rounds were twofold. Firstly, the team could draw on that display, and secondly, it was psychologically important to have that type of win in the bank.

'Like every campaign there were highs and lows. The team hit a rough patch around Christmas following on from the November internationals and things just weren't clicking. But you could see the collective will to get things back on track. With the Heineken Cup the key is getting the simple things right and pacing yourself over the course of eight months. Perhaps the team could have gotten out of the group with a bit more leeway, but the reality was that the hardships helped to define the character of the squad.

Hickie feels that before the victory in the 2009 final, the greatest performance by a Leinster team was the 41–35 away to Toulouse in the 2006 quarter-final.

'It was an incredible occasion to be a part of, probably the greatest game I was ever involved in for Leinster, but recently it began to annoy me because I always believed that we were a club capable of winning major honours, yet here we had seemingly settled for a one-off victory. It was almost as if that was the best we could have done.

'Family commitments meant that I watched the final in a quiet room in the Shelbourne Hotel while my twin sister Bairbre's wedding took place downstairs. It was an incredible feeling at the final whistle. For me there were three possible outcomes: (1) that we won the game, (2) that we lost the game and (3) extra time, which would have resulted in serious questions being asked downstairs about my absence!

'And the Leinster theme to the day was completed when Shane [Horgan] dropped by the hotel that evening, because he would know my sister for years. That was a great end to an incredible day.'

ONE EYE ON FRANCE

❝ We decided as a group that we needed to focus on the win, first and foremost. **❞**

As the New Year bells rang around him with promises of goodwill and joy, Ronan McCormack faced a doubtful time. A recurrence of a bulging disc problem flared up once more at the turn of the year and he faced into another long uncertain year.

'I had struggled to regain fitness after shoulder surgery in May 2007 and only played one match in the 2007/8 season. I started the season well, determined to make up for lost time, managing to push myself into contention for a few games, until a neck injury struck in November. The bulging disc problem improved and I was in the squad for the Castres away game, but the injury then reoccurred in January. I had no power in my left arm and had lost a lot of strength and power in my upper body.

'I spoke to Arthur Tanner and I then decided that at the age I was at, thirty-two, I wasn't going to put my body in jeopardy with a procedure that may or may not have worked. It was a very tough time for me mentally. I sat at home that month and any thoughts of being involved in a Heineken Cup final couldn't have been further from my mind. I was on the verge of retiring altogether from rugby.'

With injuries also accounting for Malcolm O'Kelly and Leo Cullen, the

LEFT: Isa Nacewa reaches for the slippery ball in Leinster's final group-stage match

ABOVE: Stephen Keogh

former Munster second-row Trevor Hogan had a chance to stake a claim alongside an in-form Devin Toner.

'An eight-day build-up can make the week seem longer, but it enabled us to get another day's recovery and we could do extra video work,' Hogan recalls. 'There were a number of meetings and obviously the issue of the bonus point was something that we discussed because a bonus-point win would guarantee us a place in the knockout stages.

'I enjoyed the build-up. On the Tuesday before the game I was assigned to speak to the Sunday press for their previews and this was a labour of love because I studied journalism and have a keen interest in the media.

'With the game so far away in the week it was a bit more relaxed because they were under less pressure with their deadlines, so it was a bit of craic. There was even time for a bit of role-reversal where I got to ask a few questions!

'Because of the longer week, and the 1 p.m. kick-off, it requires you to adjust your body clock to take into account the early start. It's more of

a struggle for someone like me, who enjoys a lie-in on the morning of matches. Instead you might be up at 8 a.m. to get a good breakfast inside you before having a plate of Bolognese or chicken and pasta two hours later.

'We decided as a group that we needed to focus on the win, first and foremost, build scores and not get stressed by the pursuit of four tries. If we forced tries, then we could leave ourselves open to unforced errors and with Wasps having to get a result down in Castres we were still in control of our destiny in the pool.

'The game itself was tough. The weather was poor but as the game went on it became increasingly clear from the reactions of the crowd that Wasps were losing, so all we had to do was concentrate on getting the result.'

It's half-time and Leinster lead 12–3 through four Felipe Contepomi penalties in wet and wild conditions.

Meanwhile, in the Stade Pierre-Antoine in Castres, Danny Cipriani has given Wasps a lifeline with a superb solo try on the stroke of half-time to reduce the deficit to four points.

ABOVE: O'Driscoll makes a break

For Leo Cullen, who ran the line as water-boy that day, it made for unbearable viewing.

'Having suffered a recurrence of a shoulder injury the week before, I found this game particularly agonizing to watch from the sidelines,' Cullen recalls. The closest analogy I could make would be to a relegation battle in football. There are different permutations cropping up once the action gets under way and you have one eye on events elsewhere.'

❝ It became increasingly clear from the reactions of the crowd that Wasps were losing, so all we had to do was concentrate on getting the result. ❞

With four minutes to go, Thomas Bouquié handed Castres their second win of the campaign with his second try of the afternoon, and the relief was palpable in the RDS as for the first time sunshine peered through the hitherto grey skyline. No bonus point would be needed.

As Rocky Elsom succinctly described the contest, 'It wasn't pretty viewing but we were fortunate that Castres defeated Wasps, which took the pressure off.'

With a quarter-final berth confirmed, the destination was the only question that remained. Later that afternoon, as all the results were compiled, Leinster's destiny was confirmed.

And once more, London was calling …

Leinster 12, Edinburgh 3
Sunday, 25 January 2009

RDS, 1 p.m.
Attendance: 18,240

LEINSTER 15: Rob Kearney, 14: Shane Horgan (Gordon D'Arcy, 53), 13: Brian O'Driscoll, 12: Felipe Contepomi, 11: Luke Fitzgerald, 10: Isa Nacewa, 9: Chris Whitaker, captain; 1: Cian Healy (Ollie le Roux, 71), 2: Bernard Jackman (John Fogarty, 68), 3: Stan Wright, 4: Trevor Hogan, 5: Devin Toner, 6: Rocky Elsom, 7: Shane Jennings, 8: Jamie Heaslip

EDINBURGH 15: Chris Paterson, 14: Andrew Turnbull, 13: Nick De Luca, 12: John Houston, 11: Jim Thompson (Ben Cairns, 67), 10: David Blair, 9: Greig Laidlaw; 1: Kyle Traynor (Gavin Kerr, 54), 2: Andrew Kelly (Steve Lawrie, 71), 3: Geoff Cross, 4: Craig Hamilton, 5: Ben Gissing, 6: Scott Newlands, 7: Simon Cross, 8: Allister Hogg, captain (Alan MacDonald, 58) (Roland Reid for MacDonald 61– 6)

REPLACEMENTS NOT USED: Stephen Keogh, Sean O'Brien, Chris Keane, Girvan Dempsey

LEINSTER SCORER: F. Contepomi (4 penalties)

EDINBURGH SCORER: C. Paterson (1 penalty)

REFEREE: Chris White (England)

'YOU CAN'T HAVE ONE WITHOUT THE OTHER …'

The section of the Main Stand in Murrayfield which housed the squad's families was the easiest to spot in Edinburgh amidst the delight, for their smiles were the ones that radiated around the stadium telling a tale of tolerance and understanding.

Yes, tolerance. For sportsmen and women are not the easiest people to live with. The higher the stakes, the greater the pressure. Behind every man, and all that. For the wives and partners, for nine months of the year, it's highs and lows, having to deal with things like loss of form, suspension and injury.

And that's as well as leading their own lives. But of course, like any other relationship, it is not a one-way street.

At lunchtime on the day of the final in the Roxburghe Hotel in the heart of Edinburgh, there was an informal gathering of friends and family of the players. The Taoiseach, Brian Cowen, acknowledged the role played by all those behind the scenes in helping to bring the team to this point.

For Stephanie O'Kelly, wife of Leinster and Ireland second-row Malcolm, this year was the culmination of the hopes and dreams generated over many years.

'The days before big games can get quite tense,' she says. 'Mal is a relaxed guy and isn't easily fazed, but he tends to keep the head down and focused on the game ahead. On the day of a home game I'd just leave him to it and give him his own space.'

Malcolm O'Kelly's younger sister Caitríona works as a masseuse with the Leinster squad, so, as Stephanie says, 'It's really a family effort. I'd say that over the course of the last ten years or so I could count on one hand the number of matches Mary and Colm [Malcolm and Catríona's parents] have missed. Speaking to the players you can tell what kind of a lift that level of support also gives them.

'The night before the Munster semi-final there was a lot of nervous energy around the house. For me this was the final. The hype had gone on for weeks. It was a chance to lay the ghosts to rest from before. For me there was also the added spice of Mal coming up against his brother-in-law' – Alan Quinlan, who is married to Stephanie's sister Ruth. 'My poor dad had to sit on the fence for the game, and that even permeated down to the colour of his clothing on that day so that there was no hint of bias. He felt he couldn't cheer for either team, even though he got his ticket from Mal, come to think of it!

'My mother's family are from Waterford while my father is from Kerry, but even though I have Munster roots I'm a Leinster girl through and through. You have to support where you live. I'd be quite adamant about things like that.

'There's great camaraderie in the group. When new players come to the club, we'd take their wife or partner out and try to help her settle in. It's not a big deal, but you'd hope that the same courtesy would be extended if the roles were reversed because it can be quite lonely moving to another country. We all get on well.

'The "Wag" label is terrible and I don't think there's any similarity between the lifestyles we lead compared to the footballers' wives or girlfriends in England. We're all independent women, some of whom are very successful in their own fields, and none of us court attention.

'Generally the wives and girlfriends would always meet up for a bit of lunch or a coffee before the game. I'd often travel with the likes of Sinead Jackman and Anne-Marie Dempsey, for example. At the final we were seated as a group right behind the tunnel and I was beside Caitríona and seated just behind Johnny Sexton's dad. At the end of the day we all want the best for the team, like the supporters do, and when the final whistle sounded we were all completely delirious. The scenes in Edinburgh airport: the craic and the singing were just a wonderful memory for all of us to savour.'

❝ The "Wag" label is terrible and I don't think there's any similarity between the lifestyles we lead compared to the footballers' wives or girlfriends in England. ❞

CHAPTER 13
SECOND-CITY SYNDROMES

❝ Everything felt right about that day. **❞**

As the national side captivated the country with only its second ever Grand Slam during the long hiatus between the group and knockout stages of the Heineken Cup, preparations were under way for the Easter Sunday quarter-final against Harlequins. Leinster gained momentum with three successive Magners League victories, away to Scarlets and Ospreys and then at home to Ulster.

For Felipe Contepomi, it was one of the most emotional periods of his career. On 12 March he announced details of his summer transfer to Toulon.

Furthermore, influential skipper Leo Cullen played 40 minutes for Blackrock College in an AIL game against Ballymena as he tried to return to full fitness after surgery on his injured sholder. 'It was my comeback from injury, the same day that Ireland were crowned Grand Slam champions and it was a bit of a blast from the past.'

Leinster's last Magners League match before the European quarter-final was against Munster, and both squads were bolstered by returning national heroes. A packed Thomond Park provided the perfect 'Test match' pressure cooker, but, despite dominating for spells in the game, Leinster were beaten by 17 points. Though naturally disappointed, the squad were far from despondent.

LEFT: Felipe Contepomi looks for space in a tight,
tense quarter-final at the Twickenham Stoop

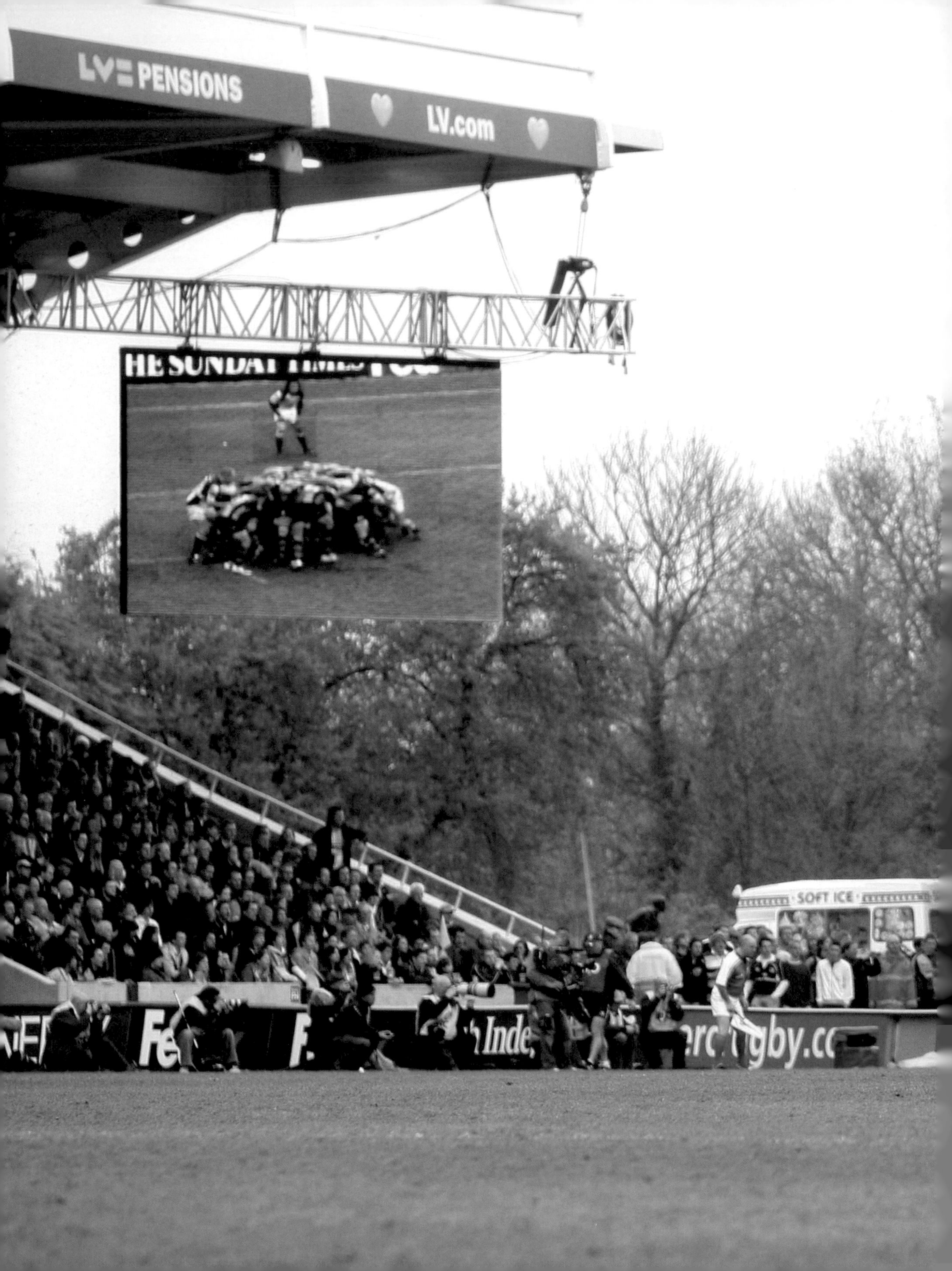
LV= PENSIONS
LV.com
HE SUNDAY TIMES
SOFT ICE

ROCKY ELSOM: 'It can be very disruptive when players leave to join international camps during the season. We regrouped during the Six Nations and carved out important victories over the Scarlets and the Ospreys away from home. By the time the Ireland players had returned from their Grand Slam win we had simplified our game-plan.'

CHRIS WHITAKER: 'As well as the game I had other things on my mind, namely my wife Alison, who was late giving birth to our third daughter. I was quite anxious going into the Harlequins game with that on my mind, but I called home regularly that day and everything was fine.'

MALCOLM O'KELLY: 'Harlequins, maybe like ourselves, suffered from capital-city syndrome. They were perceived as a team without heart, a team of glamorous flair and no real substance. But the 'Quins team we faced were young, keen and developing.'

ABOVE: Contepomi slots one of his two penalties

ROB KEARNEY: 'Everything felt right about that day. Preparations had gone well so the excitement of playing in a quarter-final outweighed any nerves. As it is I'm normally quite relaxed before games like this. Everyone approaches games differently, but I'd prefer to have a laugh and a joke right up until the time we leave the team hotel.'

SIMON KEOGH: 'It was a homecoming of sorts for me. My wife said that she was thinking of supporting 'Quins – talk about loyalty! We were both treated incredibly well during my time. It was a bit of fun and she eventually saw sense, after I wore her down! I'm still friendly with a number of the players and even some of their supporters were on to me ahead of this game.

'The night before the match my wife and I went out for dinner with Jim Evans and his wife, who used to be our neighbours. Jim was on the bench for 'Quins the following day, and I remember thinking how bizarre it was to be sitting there eating dinner ahead of the biggest game of the

season for both of our teams. We used to walk the short distance to the Stoop together before every home game. He'd be on his own tomorrow, though …'

SHANE JENNINGS: 'We came into the 'Quins game as slight favourites and that can sometimes nag at you. Teams psychologically like to go into games like this as the underdogs. They didn't have many stellar names but under Dean Richards they had a strong team ethic. We knew that we would have to set the standard on the day from our defensive foundation and it was always going to be tough.'

ROCKY ELSOM: 'Harlequins were flying in their league. They weren't the best side I've ever come up against, but they had a well-organized backline, a good set of forwards and some really effective strike players in Nick Evans, Ugo Monye and Jordan Turner-Hall.

CHRIS WHITAKER: 'Kurt has done an incredible job over the last few years on our defence and it was a backs-to-the-wall day. We didn't have a defence coach in the first year with Leinster, but his contribution has been important. A team can have all the flair in the world, but without a sound defence you won't have that added substance that wins you trophies.'

SIMON KEOGH: 'There was a sense that they were happy with their lot. That reaching the quarter-finals was the measure of their goals for the year in Europe and that their real focus was on the Premiership. They didn't have us fooled. They were on a high, and speaking to players and coaches ahead of the game they believed that it was a game that they could win.

'The subs spent the closing quarter of the match down at the far end warming up in front of the Leinster support because we spent a fair amount of time defending our lines. I remember saying to Shane Horgan, "This has to be the most nervous I've ever been in a game," and he agreed. Those moments on the bench can be excruciating because you can't change anything no matter how much you wish you could.'

MALCOLM O'KELLY: 'I've played in games in front of crowds where you could count the numbers in between scrums. We have had bigger crowds and

RIGHT: Rocky Elsom, in another towering performance, makes a clean break

maybe more vocal support, but this was the key game when the Leinster supporters inspired us to victory.'

ROB KEARNEY: 'The margins at this level are so minute that there's not much you can do when you concede penalties, or your opponents take a pop at a drop goal, both of which are out of your control. I remember standing under the posts when Evans lined up that kick and prayed to the gods that it wouldn't go over…'

ROCKY ELSOM: The slender advantage didn't come into the equation for us in the last few moments because as long as you're ahead in the game then

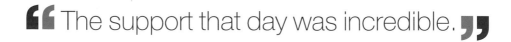 The support that day was incredible.

ABOVE: Gordon D'Arcy tries to break through the stout Harlequins defence

that's all that really matters. The problem for us at the end was in actually closing out the match, as there were a couple of knock-ons from them that were either not called by the officials or we played on.

'The support that day was incredible, and it was a phenomenal effort by them. During the post-match press conference nearly all of the attention was on the semi. I suppose it's understandable that Munster was the next big story, but as a player it's hard looking ahead when at that time you just want to take stock of what just happened and enjoy the win.'

GIRVAN DEMPSEY: 'It was one of the rare times when not one replacement was made and the entire bench really got into the game almost as supporters. The game was on a knife-edge so it was understandable that no changes were made. I distinctly remember warming up at the end of the ground every 15 or 20 minutes down where the majority of the Leinster supporters were and the reception we got was just unbelievable. It might sound strange, but it made you warm up that bit harder.

'We could see all of the drama that was unfolding with the Nick Evans "blood" substitution. We had played so well and there was a sense that they were trying to cheat us out of our place in the semis. When he lined up that kick, having come on in such controversial circumstances, you just sensed the worst, but then when the drop-goal effort fell wide in the last minute of the game there was a feeling of relief, delight and destiny.'

Earlier in the year, on St Valentine's Day, the GAA Central Council had provisionally made Croke Park available in the event of both Irish provinces qualifying for the last four. Now it was going to happen.

Having swatted aside a fancied Ospreys side 43–9 at home earlier that Easter Sunday, Munster were piping-hot favourites for the semi. As Leinster held their nerve for the narrowest of victories in London, the scene was now set.

It was to be a build-up that nobody would ever forget …

Harlequins 5, Leinster 6
Sunday, 12 April 2009

The Twickenham Stoop, 2.30 p.m.
Attendance: 12,638

HARLEQUINS: 15: Mike Brown, 14: David Strettle, 13: Gonzalo Tiesi, 12: Jordan Turner-Hall, 11: Ugo Monye, 10: Nick Evans (Chris Malone, 47) (Tom Williams, 69) (Nick Evans, 74), 9: Danny Care; 1: Ceri Jones, 2: Gary Botha, 3: Mike Ross, 4: James Percival (Jim Evans, 70), 5: George Robson, 6: Chris Robshaw, 7: Will Skinner, captain, 8: Nick Easter

LEINSTER: 15: Rob Kearney, 14: Isa Nacewa, 13: Brian O'Driscoll, 12: Gordon D'Arcy, 11: Luke Fitzgerald, 10: Felipe Contepomi, 9: Chris Whitaker; 1: Cian Healy, 2: Bernard Jackman, 3: Stan Wright, 4: Leo Cullen, captain, 5: Malcolm O'Kelly, 6: Rocky Elsom, 7: Shane Jennings, 8: Jamie Heaslip

REPLACEMENTS NOT USED: John Fogarty, Ronan McCormack, Trevor Hogan, Sean O'Brien, Simon Keogh, Girvan Dempsey, Shane Horgan

HARLEQUINS SCORER: M. Brown (1 try)

LEINSTER SCORER: F. Contepomi (2 penalties)

REFEREE: Nigel Owens (Wales)

LEFT: Nick Evans, back on the pitch after a controversial 'blood' substitution, pulls a last-minute drop-goal attempt wide

FLYING A KITE

> **" I wanted to get people talking about where they were from. "**

Walking up the Clonliffe Road towards Irish sport's great cathedral at lunchtime on 2 May, Reggie Corrigan must have felt a hint of déjà vu.

As the sun kissed the lightest of breezes around lunchtime, an ill wind was forming in the shape of a French photographer, gathering colour-feature shots, who asked that he and his group, including his wife Frieda, pose for a photograph. Corrigan, who had only recently lost the distinction of being Leinster's most-capped player to Malcolm O'Kelly, was happy to oblige, before the snapper informed him that they were the first overtly Leinster group he had encountered!

'Here we go again,' Corrigan mused despondently.

In his *Sunday Times* column the week previously, he had introduced the 'Lunster' – a cowardly creature from the east who suckles, proverbially speaking, from the teat of his or her southern cousin's success.

'I had had enough,' he recalls. 'I wanted to get people talking about where they were from and to stir people into backing their own.'

The column provoked intrigue and comment. As the requests came in inviting him to substantiate his argument, he was happy with the furore he had created. Each night that week he sat back in his Wicklow home with his

ABOVE: Reggie Corrigan celebrates with his Leinster teammates, 2002

baby boy Nathan and smiled. He had achieved exactly what he intended. Game on.

The joy that followed Leinster's victory was an altogether different feeling than that which he felt walking off the field in Lansdowne Road after 72 minutes in 2006, the last time the two sides met in a European semi-final.

'The hype for this game was similar to 2006,' he says. 'We had come off the back of a fantastic win in Toulouse and went into the game as favourites. The roles had reversed now and the pressure in 2009 was all on Munster. They came in on the back of an exceptional attacking display over the Ospreys, while the perception was that Leinster had barely scraped through away to Harlequins.

'I had a good feeling all week. Leinster flew under the radar into the knockout stages. There were lots of grumblings, it had been an up-and-down journey to date and nobody really gave the team a prayer.

'It sounds simple, but the key to this competition is getting out of your pool. Leinster did that and then faced a team they really knew very little about. That was the acid test because it highlighted the simple point about this team: that nothing had come easy. That we had earned the right to be here.'

CHAPTER FOURTEEN

CHAPTER 15
REDEMPTION

Coin toss, it falls on heads. Leinster will change in the home dressing-room. In the week before the all-Ireland clash in the European semi-final, this amounted to headline news.

There were tales of homecomings from every corner of the world. Unofficial Leinster Supporters Clubs from Penn State University and the University of Oregon were flying the flag for the province along the east and west coasts of the USA. Other gatherings of Leinster people, expats or first-time enthusiasts, sprang up in bars and clubs in Dubai, Pakistan, Bahrain, Malaysia, Australia, New Zealand, Argentina, Canada and Alaska.

But this was parochial to the core. It was about two communities, two traditions, two provinces going head to head in the most unique set of circumstances in the history of Irish sport.

This was about parishes such as Bellewstown and Ferns, Carlingford and Kilcock, Tullow and Clontarf, Ballymahon and Enniskerry, supporting their local heroes.

Rocky Elsom, from the parish of Melbourne, recalls: 'There was obviously a huge historical backdrop to the semi, but that side of things didn't really affect me. What I do know is that it was good going into the game as heavy

LEFT: Early substitute Jonathan Sexton exhorts his team-mates against a backdrop of Munster red

underdogs. When people say that you're going to lose and that you haven't a hope of winning it doesn't sit well. It was certainly an occasion that I could enjoy maybe more than some of the other guys; for one thing I didn't have a list of friends or family who were plaguing me for tickets!

'There was obviously a lot of negative feeling towards us in the media, but how you react is what's important. If you believe what's being said then you're going to run into problems.'

Gordon D'Arcy, meanwhile, had been here before and was determined not to get distracted. 'I was lucky in that I could escape most of the build-up. It was nice when people came up to wish you well, but I'd say 90 per cent of that week, outside of things like team meetings and training, went over my head. It seemed like everybody had an opinion on the match, but I hardly read the papers or listened to the sports shows.'

In the week preceding the semi, the Grand Slam-winning Ireland squad were invited to the Phoenix Park for a reception with Mary McAleese, Uachtarán na hÉireann.

'The strangest aspect of the preparations was the Ireland squad visit to Áras an Uachtaráin to mark the Grand Slam,' says Malcolm O'Kelly. 'Don't get me wrong, the lads all get on well and there's always great craic between the provinces when we come together, but that day, a little under a fortnight before the biggest club match of my career, was weird.

'I've obviously regular interaction with Quinny [Alan Quinlan] through my wife Stephanie and her sister Ruth, but it's a case of the great unsaid on weeks like that.'

Chris Whitaker recalls, 'I remembered the huge significance of Croke Park first opening up for rugby, so I was especially excited to be playing there because it was going to be a once-in-a-lifetime opportunity. As a foreign player you realized the history behind the whole occasion pretty quickly.'

" I remember speaking to Shane Horgan that Monday morning and he was so pumped up he would have played the game there and then. "

Everywhere Isa Nacewa looked that week, the semi-final hit home. He needed a crash course in Irish history and he spoke to a man who knew a thing or two about the ground.

'As a foreign player coming into a new culture you try to soak up as much information as possible,' he says. 'I remember speaking to Shane Horgan that Monday morning and he was so pumped up he would have played the game there and then. You could see how much the game meant to him and you can only feed off that passion.'

Devin Toner drew the short straw to face the media that week. Having been reared on the feats of the Royal County in a venue he hoped one day to grace, he strode into the Bective clubhouse that Monday night with a sense of pride and purpose. The numbers present struck him. His pupils momentarily dilated, he paused, took a breath and got his game face on, five days before required.

'When I was told I was up I remember thinking, "Are you serious?!" But as it turned out it was grand. They all just wanted to talk to Sexto anyway,' Toner says.

'To step out in Croke Park, the scene of all the great Meath games that I'd been to over the years, was incredible. Footballers like Trevor Giles, Graham Geraghty and Tommy Dowd were heroes to me growing up. Then to have messages of support from the likes of Robbie Keane, Ken Doherty and Meath's own Sean Boylan ahead of the semi gave you a nice lift.'

The question of Felipe Contepomi's temperament for the big stage sparked debate – 'Target Contepomi' screamed one headline ahead of the encounter – but the attention was water off a duck's back for the Argentinian. 'Over the last few years I spoke to Cheiks about my temperament and there's no doubting that at times I was too "Latin" during games, too fired up and prone to losing the plot. Even *The Rugby Club* on Sky had run a feature claiming that if teams targeted me then they would beat us, but the highlights they used were from several years back. In that sense I was quite calm. Perhaps old age gave me that!'

Messages for the Leinster squad as a whole came in from great Leinster sporting and entertainment figures past and present: Wexford footballer Matty Forde, Dublin footballer Ciaran Whelan, boxer Katie Taylor, former world snooker champion Ken Doherty, businessman (and former Leinster and Ireland star) Sir Anthony O'Reilly, Dublin football legend Brian Mullins,

> **❝** I've always listened to senior players as a captain and sometimes you need to rely on experience. There was a need to reiterate that chances like this didn't come along too often. **❞**

former Meath football manager Sean Boylan, international footballers Kevin Doyle and Robbie Keane, and singer Ronan Keating, among others.

GIRVAN DEMPSEY: 'Talking to my parents in Offaly, they were telling me about all the Leinster flags outside the pubs, shops and houses, and my wife Anne-Marie said it was the same in Tallaght where she works. You could feel the sense of occasion building and everyone from around Leinster seemed to be rooting for us. Training had gone well, by and large, but I had a scare during the Tuesday session in the RDS when I suffered a Grade 1 hamstring tear.

'I was seen in the Sports Clinic in Santry that afternoon and I had almost resigned myself to missing the semi that Saturday. It was a horrible feeling. To compound matters the doctor who was treating me, Dr Eanna Falvey, was a former Munster team doctor! He gave me an injection and I was very sore the next day, but the pain receded and I recovered sufficiently to be named on the bench. When you come so close to missing a game you're just delighted to be passed fit.'

BRIAN O'DRISCOLL: 'After the captain's run in Croke Park on the Thursday, Shane and I had a word with Leo because I felt that maybe we needed to pull things in. Something that's an important aspect of the team is that if one of us feels that something needs to be done or said, then he'll do it. I've always listened to senior players as a captain and sometimes you need to rely on experience. There was a need to reiterate that chances like this didn't come along too often.

'Once we chatted I felt a lot happier about how we were mentally. Preparations had gone well and not many of the lads seemed to be overly fussed about the hype that was going on. In the fortnight before the game I didn't read one newspaper and whenever there were pundits talking on

the radio about the game I turned it off because you can become clouded in your thoughts by certain people, outside of the squad, who have never been in that position. I felt good coming into the game; we were focused and we were ready.'

SHANE HORGAN: 'It was really exciting to be in the ground on the Thursday. The sun was shining and the pitch was perfect, but the session was nervous. Afterwards I remember Leo reiterating that we had done the hard work in the months previously and that we were physically and mentally prepared.'

LEO CULLEN: 'It was unusual to get the whole squad together for the captain's run on the Thursday, but it felt disjointed somehow and both Shane and Drico asked to hold a short meeting in Riverview to get greater clarity on our game-plan. Last-minute nerves are normal, but these are two players who wouldn't say something like this unless they meant it. Those words stood us well going into Saturday.

'On the day before the game I usually live the life of a hermit and the largest part of the day is spent dropping off tickets. This Friday I had other matters to attend to, namely a physio session in the morning followed by the pre-match press conference in Croke Park. The one thing that struck me on the way to the ground was the sense of blue in the streets around the stadium. Then when you saw the flags all around the ground it sent a shiver down my spine. Little things like that build momentum and I know that there was a big effort made internally to turn the ground blue. The main question from the press corps was how we were going to beat Munster. You could sense a kind of defeatism in some of the questions, but we were confident …'

JOHN FOGARTY: 'I remember my first visit to Croke Park, aged ten. My home county, Tipperary, lost by a point to Galway in the All-Ireland hurling semi-final, the likes of which I had never seen before. I remember leaving the ground that day in 1988 with my late father Denis and older brother Damian and thinking that it would be a dream come true to one day step out on to the field. In the run-up to the semi it seemed as though most of the country didn't give us a chance. We'd lost to Munster twice already this year, so that helped to develop a kind of siege mentality from within our camp. There was the added incentive of playing against former team-mates who have become friends, and of course my younger brother Denis! We had faced each other twice that season, in an "A" game in Donnybrook and in Thomond Park a few weeks previously when he came on as a sub and

❝ Shane and Drico asked to hold a short meeting in Riverview to get greater clarity on our game-plan. Last-minute nerves are normal, but these are two players who wouldn't say something like this unless they meant it. Those words stood us well going into Saturday. **❞**

scored. There is no bad feeling there between us, but we are very competitive and bragging rights are important at home.'

SHANE JENNINGS: 'I went to a Gaelic-playing primary school called St Colmcille's in Knocklyon and I lived beside Ballyboden St Enda's GAA club, but that was the extent of my Gaelic career, though I've always enjoyed watching the Dubs. So the day before the game I visited the Croke Park museum to get a feel for the history of the stadium. You could feel the buzz around Dorset Street and the Clonliffe Road and I did feed off that. There was a woman working behind the counter who engaged in a bit of small talk and she asked me if I was going to the semi. I guarantee that she would have known one of the Munster boys had they come in and that said to me that nobody, even in our own hometown, was giving us a chance.'

BERNARD JACKMAN: 'I've a habit whereby I like to go out of the tunnel second in line behind the captain. Sometimes Stan has notions of jumping in ahead of me so I have to race to beat him to it! Psychologically it helps me prepare, almost as if to say, "Right, you're here now. The onus is on you to play well ..." There was a pause of what seemed like an eternity as we lined up in the tunnel alongside the Munster team. The crowds rose to their feet ahead of us and I remembered something Ciaran Whelan, the Dublin footballer, had said about Croke Park taking your breath away on match days. I knew what he meant.'

STAN WRIGHT: 'In the tunnel it's Leo up front and then the front row; usually Birch, Cian, CJ or myself. I know Birch likes to get in second so I like to wind him up. Personally I think he just wants to get on the TV! But that day, especially as I knew everyone back home in Rarotonga would be watching, I was determined and leaving the dressing-room I said to myself "Not today, Birch"...'

SHANE HORGAN: 'When Croke Park first opened its doors to other sports no one could have envisaged that a day would come where two Irish teams, one as the reigning European champions, in a year when Ireland had won a Grand Slam, would face each other. It was an incredible game on so many levels. The local familiarity and tribalism that you see in the GAA made it feel like a kind of championship final.'

ROB KEARNEY: 'The water-boy has an important role on match days, communicating messages from the coaching staff to the players as well as delivering drinks. Realistically I knew that I had no chance of being fit for this game after being out with mumps, but I wanted to contribute to the team as best I could on the day.

'You're kneeling on the touchline waiting to run on at any moment and I was more wound up for this game than any other I'd ever played in. You have all this energy and you can't use it and it was frustrating. You can communicate messages, but deep down you know that the players are ultimately left to their own devices and responsible for their actions.'

MALCOLM O'KELLY: 'I remember taking in the atmosphere in Croker during the warm-up and with all the red around I said to myself, "This is now an away match." Then what happens? We come out into the tunnel and then the blue just hit you. I recall thinking, "Typical Dubs crowd, always leaving it until the last minute …"'

ROCKY ELSOM: 'I always felt that we had a good side, as did they, and it was a case of whatever happens on the day, happens. One of the key messages from the coaches that week was that we weren't to worry if things didn't go right. What I have learned about Leinster is that we play our best footy when we're instinctive.'

CIAN HEALY: 'I appreciate every minute on the pitch and for me to lose my composure and get sin-binned in such a big game for me and the team was frustrating. Munster, John Hayes, Croke Park – I wanted to spend every second on the pitch.

'I don't think the incident had anything to do with the lack of big-game experience or my age. Even the most professional and experienced people can slip up. I'm very lucky to be part of a team that has the strength, even with 14 men, to keep the scoreboard ticking over.

'The guilt factor kicked in when Jenno had to be replaced come scrum time, but having such a talented and experienced player as Ronnie to come on and dominate his position was comforting. I tried not to lose focus when in the bin, reciting lineouts in my head and thinking of plays. That really stood me well when the ten minutes were up – I was ready to play again.'

ABOVE: Chris Whitaker
goes airborne to
provide quick ball

SHANE JENNINGS: 'It was probably a blessing in disguise that Cian got sin-binned when he did because I suffered a blow to the head in the first five minutes and I was struggling. Ronnie came on for me as we needed a front-row replacement and thankfully Trevor Hogan came down from the stand and went through some of the calls with me. That time helped me …'

LEO CULLEN: 'One of the more notable moments from the game, which stands out more than anything, was when Stan took the high ball in the first half. It was like time had stood still and all of a sudden the ball was in his hands. Everybody was shocked, himself especially. I don't think he even knew that he had caught it until he looked down at his hands and saw the ball. The look of fear-cum-surprise-cum-delight on his face said it all.'

STAN WRIGHT: 'I was stunned … I always drop high balls in training and when the ball fell into my hands I was shocked because I didn't know what to do. Then it registered, "Well done, Stan. You gotta run now!"

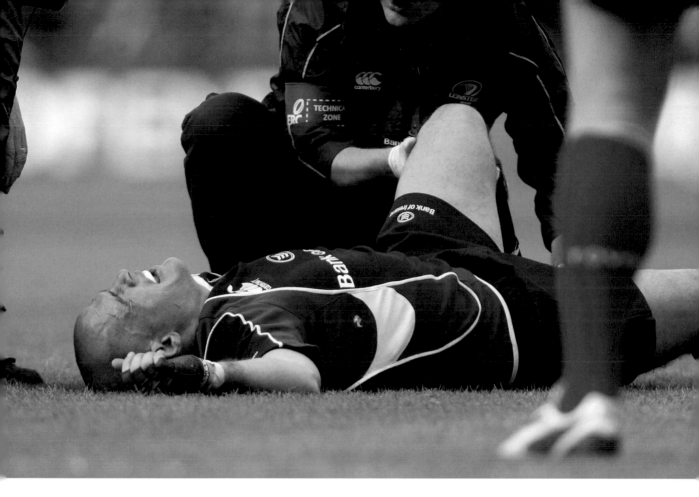

ISA NACEWA: 'I'm really close friends with Dougie Howlett and earlier in the week there was the odd silly text flying around between us. He's a great guy and someone you can really depend on. Unfortunately that expands to his rugby prowess on the field so when he made a break down the left wing in the second half, there was no way that I could let him pass. For one thing, I'd have never heard the end of it! I threw myself at his ankles and prayed that he fell over. Thankfully, he did.'

FELIPE CONTEPOMI: 'Coming into the game I felt I was in the best possible shape physically and mentally. The fitness team had done a superb job in ensuring that we were peaking at the right time. As the days approached I felt we were ready. The aim from the kick-off was to kick it high, chase and tackle hard. We were on top and the early drop goal meant that our tails were up.

'A quarter of the way into the match and we're flying in the biggest club game in history against our oldest rivals in front of the largest crowd in

CHAPTER FIFTEEN

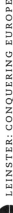

ABOVE: Jonathan Sexton came on for Contepomi, and his first task was to kick a tricky penalty – which he slotted coolly between the posts

Croke Park. Then, just five minutes later, my game is over. I took the ball and tried to step inward but my foot got stuck in the ground and the next thing I heard a snap and all of a sudden my Leinster playing career became a memory.'

JONATHAN SEXTON: 'I had played a lot of Magners League games since January so I was quite happy with my form coming into the game. I remembered thinking about the 2006 semi-final in Lansdowne Road and though I wasn't at the game itself I was struck by the crowd and the large Munster presence that day. I was quite nervous before the game because it was without a doubt the biggest of my career.

'We started well but after around 10 minutes I went down to the touchline and got myself prepped because Felipe had taken a bang on his wrist and it looked like he was coming off.

'He's one of the toughest players you'll come across, someone I have huge respect for, and even though I wanted to get out there I didn't want

RIGHT: Rocky Elsom whistles past David Wallace

him to come off injured because he is also a world-class player. There was a degree of uncertainty as to whether he'd continue so I hung around for a few more minutes because he didn't look too comfortable, but eventually I returned to the dugout. Next thing I knew he was down and this time I was coming on ...'

RICHIE MURPHY: 'Felipe set the tempo with a string of excellent kicks and a superb drop goal. By the time Johnny came on he was immediately faced with a penalty in front of a full house. Of course you're anxious but any kicker is used to that. As a kicking coach you just try to prepare for different scenarios and practice makes perfect.

'When that first kick went over I was very relieved because this was a big moment, when he was put on the spot as the main place-kicker on the pitch in the biggest game of his career where the pressure was truly on his shoulders. I could hardly bear to watch. It's to his immense credit that he went on to make such a telling contribution that day.'

JONATHAN SEXTON: 'It's hard when a team-mate comes off injured. My first thought was "Poor Felipe", but then came the realization that I had to come on and do a job. For me that immediately meant having to take a penalty. You run on to the pitch, notice the crowd and then I hollered at Hago [Johnny O'Hagan] for bringing out the wrong kicking tee!

'I've known Hago nearly all my life, right from the time I used to hang around the ground in Donnybrook all those years back to see my father play for Bective. Johnny's a great character, a hugely popular figure in the dressing-room, and I felt comfortable with him doing the kicking tee for me. But I stored that moment in the memory bank for later that evening when I hoped that we could laugh about it. Thankfully my first input was a positive one and it went on from there.'

" My first thought was "Poor Felipe", but then came the realization that I had to come on and do a job. "

GORDON D'ARCY: 'When Felipe went down injured it was hard because we didn't know what the extent of the injury was. But you have to pick yourself up and move on, because in games of that intensity any momentary lapse in concentration can be devastating. Looking at the high camera view of our first try, all you can see is fellas in blue shirts running all these intricate lines.

'I haven't scored that many tries, and it's usually Briano showing a bit of pace on the outside, but he did well in the build-up. He drew in two defenders and then the line that Isa took was incredible. It cut a massive hole in the Munster defence and so I followed him and took the pass and could see the try-line in sight. Lukey was calling me in support, but there was no way you'd pass!'

JONATHAN SEXTON: 'Darce's try was a key moment in the game. When he scored I let out a roar of delight more than anything. It was a split-second thing and when I saw the papers the following day I regretted it because

ABOVE: Luke Fitzgerald looks to touch down for Leinster's second try after an intricate move carved the Munster defence open

I have great respect for Ronan O'Gara, who was right there. I also have a lot of family in Munster who would have had to put up with some comments after the game. All players make comments during a match, on both sides, but when the final whistle sounds you leave it out on the pitch. One of my frustrations from the day was the impression that the photo left. I didn't enjoy the picture or watching that footage on TV and regret it because I would prefer people to remember the performance itself.'

LUKE FITZGERALD: 'The [second] try was a very special moment for me and I was lucky to get on the end of some fantastic team play. Many of the plaudits went to me, which I was very pleased with, but it was down to clinical handling from Brian and Shane, which enabled me – in a very tight game – to have a one-on-one with the fullback.'

BRIAN O'DRISCOLL: 'The [third] try was one of those opportunities that can either come along or you can end up with egg on your face. We were under

RIGHT: Malcolm O'Kelly grabs a lineout ball ahead of Munster captain Paul O'Connell

ABOVE: Girvan Dempsey contratulates Brian O'Driscoll on his long-distance intercept try, which put Leinster out of sight

the cosh after a spell of Munster pressure and I had spotted something in the backline, which I took a chance on. Paulie [O'Connell] is often a preferred ball carrier and there's a certain mannerism that Rog [Ronan O'Gara] has whereby I knew that if I got myself in the right place at the right time that I could possibly benefit. On another day it might have found Donncha [O'Callaghan].

'Jogging back to the half-way line after it I was shattered but there was still an element of nerves because I knew that Munster had the wherewithal to come back from a 19-point deficit. They've pulled rabbits out of the hat so many times before…'

JOHN FOGARTY: 'Strangely, I had been here at the semi-final stages before with Munster, back in 2002. That year we beat Castres in the Stade de la Méditerranée in Béziers. Munster lost the final that year to Leicester. Obviously coming up against my brother Denis was a strange experience and I have to admit feeling a gush of pride when I saw him run on to the field.

NEXT PAGE: The Leinster
defence spent a lot
of time in the shadow
of the posts in the
second half, but
Munster never broke
through

'That feeling soon dissipated when I got my emotions back in check. It still is for me a highlight to play on the same pitch as my brother in such a big game. Simon Keogh and I had this thing all season where we'd ask each other when do the nerves kick in and for whatever reason it was the 55th minute.

'Next thing I knew Birch was down and I knew my chance was coming. I ran on to the field and my first touch of the ball was at a lineout. Normally you'd get a nice easy one first up to the number two jumper, but Leo called one over the top to Rocky and chuckled – "Best of luck with that one!" His calmness relaxed me and thankfully the ball flew and hit the target.'

LEO CULLEN: 'It was only when Quinny came over to speak to me at the end of the game that I remembered the incident and there was no issue. I'd have liked to have seen him go on the Lions tour. It was just a shame it happened.'

It's easy to get caught up in the moment of celebration, to lose your focus and forget that there is one more mountain still to climb. As the clock ran past the 80th minute, scenes of jubilation were met by moments of clarity.

Swarms of players and officials embraced and stood out on the terrain, drinking in the moment.

As delighted as Gordon D'Arcy was to savour the win, the tone of the celebrations was of calm and clarity.

'Some of the lads were wary about applauding the crowd at the end, but it was a small acknowledgement for all their support. Sitting in the changing-room after the game there was a feeling of, *Well done, lads. See you in training on Monday*. It was vital at that stage that we kept our heads.'

For John Fogarty it was a bittersweet moment. 'We were delighted but calm because the ultimate prize was worth more than beating Munster. I remember hugging Denis and he just said how happy he was for me.

'I grew up in the Munster squad with the likes of Rog and Donners with Cork Con, and Denis Leamy, who's also from Tipp. They were pretty down about things, which is understandable, but were gracious and wished us the best.'

The following morning Malcolm O'Kelly awoke and arose, for an expectant canine had different business to attend to. It was almost as

if the cocker spaniel was in on some big secret.

'There's a group of people I've gotten to know over the last year or so, different groups of people united by the one pastime, walking our dogs in Dodder Park.

'The morning after the game I was taking Poppy around, and the next thing I knew a group of the dog-walkers broke into a spontaneous round of applause. It was quite nice and humbling, if a little bizarre …'

Munster 6, Leinster 25
Saturday, 2 May 2009

Croke Park, 5.30 p.m.
Attendance: 82,208

MUNSTER: 15: Paul Warwick (Barry Murphy, 66), 14: Doug Howlett, 13: Keith Earls (Denis Hurley, 78), 12: Lifeimi Mafi, 11: Ian Dowling, 10: Ronan O'Gara, 9: Peter Stringer (Mike Prendergast, 74); 1: Marcus Horan, 2: Jerry Flannery (Denis Fogarty, 71), 3: John Hayes (Tony Buckley, 67), 4: Donncha O'Callaghan (Mick O'Driscoll, 74), 5: Paul O'Connell, captain, 6: Alan Quinlan, 7: David Wallace, 8: Denis Leamy (Niall Ronan, 66)

LEINSTER: 15: Isa Nacewa, 14: Shane Horgan, 13: Brian O'Driscoll (Girvan Dempsey 37–8), 12: Gordon D'Arcy, 11: Luke Fitzgerald (Girvan Dempsey, 59), 10: Felipe Contepomi (Jonathan Sexton, 25), 9: Chris Whitaker, 1: Cian Healy, 2: Bernard Jackman (John Fogarty, 63), 3: Stan Wright, 4: Leo Cullen, captain (Devin Toner, 80), 5: Malcolm O'Kelly, 6: Rocky Elsom, 7: Shane Jennings (Ronan McCormack, 19–27) (Sean O'Brien, 73), 8: Jamie Heaslip

REPLACEMENT NOT USED: Simon Keogh

MUNSTER SCORERS: R. O'Gara (2 penalties)

LEINSTER SCORERS: B. O'Driscoll / G. D'Arcy / L. Fitzgerald (1 try each), J. Sexton (2 conversions, 1 penalty), F. Contepomi (1 drop goal)

REFEREE: Nigel Owens (Wales)

LEFT ABOVE: Shane Jennings celebrates after the final whistle

LEFT BELOW: John Fogarty, left, with Cian Healy, punches the air

CHAPTER 16
THE PROMISED LAND

❝ After the Munster game the temptation would have been for the players to maybe wind down and let off a bit of steam, but the feeling straight afterwards was that our job was undone. **❞**

With the Magners League title already known to be heading to Munster, Leinster faced into the final fortnight of the domestic season knowing that they could rotate the squad and thus keep the majority of the starting squad under wraps for the final.

For Rob Kearney, who had missed the semi-final, it was a final opportunity to push himself into contention after bravely battling back from illness.

'The majority of the match 22 for the final were given the week off for an away trip to the Dragons, which was our last game of the Magners League campaign. This was a massively important game for me because it was my last chance to stake a claim for the final by getting 80 minutes under my belt. My focus ahead of the Dragons was on building up my strength and putting on the weight I'd lost through illness.

'I knew deep down that the form of the back three was so good in the previous weeks that it was unlikely the coaches would change a winning combination, but you have to keep the head up. Playing in Rodney Parade was also a special day because as well as a host of academy players making their first senior starts, it was also my younger brother David's debut.'

> **❝** I knew deep down that the form of the back three was so good in the previous weeks that it was unlikely the coaches would change a winning combination, but you have to keep the head up. **❞**

With the Dragons match out of the way, the build-up to the European final could begin.

While Leicester were slugging it out on their way to the Guinness Premiership title in Twickenham during the previous week, Shane Jennings was busy reacquainting himself with some old friends.

'I was disappointed for Bob Casey that London Irish lost the Premiership final. We're good friends and he's someone who has put so much effort into the game over the years, but a part of me was delighted that Leicester won the title the week before. The fact that our lead-up time for the final was that bit longer was an advantage for us. They had only a week to prepare.

'No matter how hard you try, you can't have a complete detachment from clubs where you once played. I still have very close friends there. Guys like Sam Vesty and Dan Hipkiss were on at the start of the week sending texts like "If you win can I see your medal?" They were always going to be dangerous opponents because when it comes to the business end of the season they're always around. Training was sharp that week. Mentally I knew that it was going to be very tough for them to sustain another big week because the finish to the Premiership season had been so intense.

'We, on the other hand, had the luxury of resting our whole starting line-up in our last league game of the season the week before the final. I suppose that comes down to the "match-hardened or rested" debate. Were we fresher? I don't know. But we can't have been that much more so because there was only a kick of a ball between us in the end.'

Bernard Jackman, meanwhile, sat down to write his closing thoughts for the season. He thought of journeys past and of his own path to a European final. For him it began in Newbridge College, the Kildare school which had helped to produce four of the leading protagonists.

'There was a lot of talk that week about the Newbridge College connection on both teams, Jamie and I with Leinster and Geordy [Geordan

Murphy] and Johne Murphy with Leicester,' Jackman recalls.

'The media latched on to that angle and it was nice for the school to get a bit of reflected credit because it was there that we learned our trade. The *Evening Herald* even managed to source a photo from the school annual from the years each of us graduated.

'They published a photo of me in my blazer with a silly-looking grin and a full head of red hair. I hadn't seen that photo in years!'

For Cian Healy, messages of support, some from the unlikeliest of sources, were a constant reminder of the magnitude of the game at stake. 'In the lead-up to the quarters, semis and final, I received a startling number of cards, texts and well-wishers calling to the house – even avid Munster fans! Old coaches from minis in Clontarf, several of my teachers from Belvedere, and Ollie Campbell was often in touch, texting me messages of encouragement and wishing me luck.'

Coming off the back of leading Ireland to the Grand Slam, Brian O'Driscoll and his provincial colleagues were relishing the high-intensity finale. The bigger the game, the more composed the group became.

'The squad were very relaxed coming into the final,' says O'Driscoll. 'The funny thing about these bigger games is that you're never as nervous when you're involved than when you're not. When you're in the mix, it's just another big game.

'Of course there were bigger crowds, larger media interest and things but so many of the games we play in have so much at stake nowadays that you tend not to differentiate between them.'

Kurt McQuilkin recalls: 'After the Munster game the temptation would have been for the players to maybe wind down and let off a bit of steam, but the feeling straight afterwards was that our job was undone. People would come up to you on the street or down the shops and want to talk about the next game and it gave you a lift to think that so many people had confidence in the team.'

As captain, Leo Cullen projected a cool façade. He had been here before, though his memories from the final two years previously with Leicester were tainted. A flood of good-luck messages from friends and family streamed through that week. One particular note struck a chord.

'I got a message ahead of the game from Johnny Magee, the captain of the Kilmacud Crokes side who won the All-Ireland Senior club title earlier

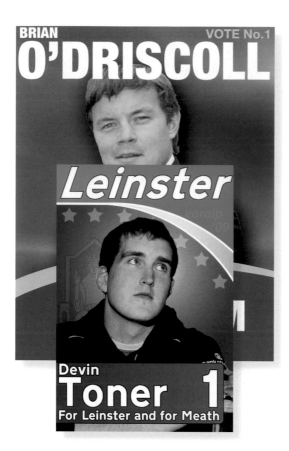

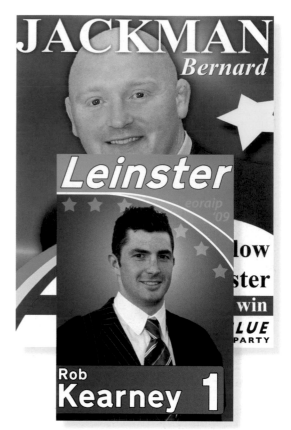

in the year. I played for a brief spell with my friend Tom Keating around the age of fifteen for a year.

'Was I a good player? Well, I scored two goals a game so if you'd call that good then I suppose … Just kidding. Let's just say I definitely took the correct sporting path!'

The run-up to the final coincided with local and European elections, and as the team gathered in Riverview ahead of the coach journey to Dublin Airport Gordon D'Arcy noticed mock 'Blue Party', 'Fianna Blue' and 'Fine Laighin' election posters carrying images of the players. He grinned at the posters, which had him down as the candidate 'for Wexford and for Leinster': 'It's funny, but I never knew I was running for political office!'

For Bernard Jackman the practical joke sparked a different reaction. 'We were on our way to the airport and a few texts started coming through from lads I was in primary school with, asking me which party I was running for and what they could do to help. I'd love to be able to say they were acting the eejit, but sadly they missed the joke …'

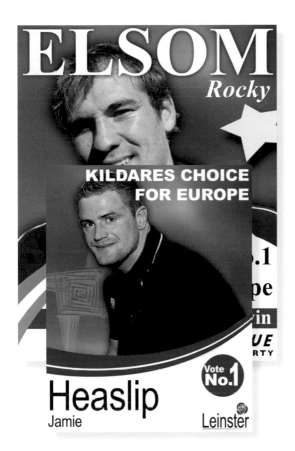

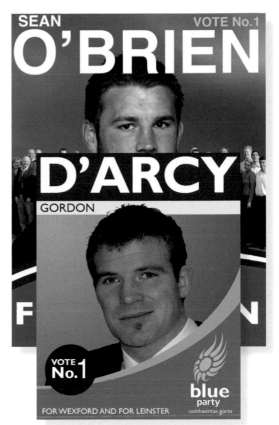

The team were whisked through the departure gates, thus avoiding the thousands of supporters travelling over to the Scottish capital via Liverpool, London, Newcastle and even Stockholm that Friday.

For Rocky Elsom the week of the match started with an incident which he could have done without. As he drove through the junction at Donnybrook Church on his way to training, his car was struck by a van that had run a red light.

'It was scary for a moment and I took a bit of a blow to the head but all the airbags went off, so I was okay, though the car was a write-off,' Elsom says. Also, my knee was a real concern in the build-up, so when I got the all-clear later that week I could relax and look forward to the game.'

'Pulling into Murrayfield for the final captain's run I was greeted by an unusual sight – a forty-foot image of myself on the back of the North Stand. It was slightly surreal and I looked quite stressed in the photo. The boys got more of a laugh out of it than I did, that's for sure!

'We went through our captain's run, which was more of a walk around,

and it was back to the hotel for a meal and put the feet up. The weather that day was the best I've ever experienced in Edinburgh. Our hotel was located a few miles outside the city and it was very tranquil, overlooking a golf course, so I spent a lot of the time talking to the guys and relaxing.

'Jenno is probably the perfect room-mate for me. He doesn't snore, for one thing. He's incredibly neat and everything he has is packed to precision. I have busted my nose a few times so there's a fair chance that people like me are inclined to snore in our sleep. It's an occupational hazard!

'We would have spoken about the game, but the danger about doing that can be when you start dwelling on hypothetical scenarios. You get anxious and that makes your own prep that bit harder and in my experience that can happen a lot with younger players.'

'How would Rocky describe me as a room-mate?' asks Shane Jennings with a grin. 'Probably anal, neat, on time, a clean freak … I like to have an ice bath and have everything packed and ready to go before we leave for a ground. He sleeps up to two minutes before we leave the team hotel.'

While the rest of the team returned to the team hotel, Contepomi stayed on with Sexton for his kicking practice in Murrayfield to offer support. 'In rugby you can always play a part, even when you're not directly involved. At the captain's run I asked Johnny if he wanted me to stay and he said yes. For me I couldn't imagine going to training and practising our kicking without him, and maybe it was the same for him.

'Ordinarily I would have been tucked up in bed early, but as I wasn't playing later that night I went into town and met Dan Carter for dinner, as a mutual sponsor of ours had invited him over to the game. Even though he had no direct involvement in the game, the magnitude of the occasion the next day wasn't lost on him.'

Later that evening, kicking coach Richie Murphy reflected on matters and knew that Sexton was ready. 'Once the rest of the team had returned to the hotel after the session on the Friday, I stayed behind with Johnny as normal and Felipe was also there for support. That time can be important for kickers because you can just get on with your own preparations without

any distractions. Sometimes kickers will want shorter or longer sessions; you kind of take direction from them.

'The day before the game there were one or two small bad habits creeping into his technique. For example, he was dropping his head on strike and that was affecting his posture. Once they were addressed he was flying. It's important in the days before the game to go through the kicker's usual routine.

'The key words are "tall" and "target-line" – stay tall and kick down the target-line. The thing about being the kicker is that you are used to being under pressure. Over the last season we re-created different psychological scenarios with the kickers which they responded to very well. Over the course of a week he will probably spend three hours practising outside of sessions and, like lineout throwing or accuracy in passing, you get out of it what you put in.'

Jonathan Sexton roomed with Luke Fitzgerald that evening and he also felt that preparations had gone soundly. 'Richie came in at the start of the season and put a structure on practice. I remember a spell of six games playing for St Mary's College and Leinster A during my Academy years when I didn't miss a kick and he was one of the coaches back then with Colly McEntee. That gave me great confidence this year, knowing I had someone who knew me well, and the support I got from him and all the coaches has really helped me.

'I must have kicked hundreds of balls that week, and Richie was there for every one of them along with Enda McNulty, the team psychologist. Felipe had some great words of encouragement for me. He said: "If you make decisions for the good of the team you'll do well." And, "Go out there and trust your own instincts."

'I slept okay the night before but leaving the hotel was a relief because I was so nervous, constantly thinking over and over about the game. I couldn't believe the support on the way to the ground. There were rumours that week that the Munster supporters were going to be there in force and cheering for Leicester, but the sea of blue on the streets of Edinburgh gave you an incredible feeling.'

MICHAEL CHEIKA: 'Leicester had targeted us in the previous year over in Welford Road. They probably felt that we were a soft touch, and we talked about that in the build-up.

LEFT: Gordon D'Arcy tries to fight his way through the stiff Leicester defence

PREVIOUS PAGE:
Jonathan Sexton hits
an audacious drop goal
from the halfway line to
put Leinster up 6–3

'As we approached the final leg of the season we cut down on things like the captain's run and our trainers did a superb job in keeping the players fresh. In the build-up to the final we used a lot of the colour footage of our supporters at the 'Quins game as a source of inspiration. Then to see the numbers that had travelled to Edinburgh on the day of the final was incredible.'

REGGIE CORRIGAN: 'The final was an incredible occasion. A group of a dozen or so Corrigans travelled from Dublin on the Friday and it was a fairly anxious week trying to sort out flights, tickets and accommodation. On the day of the game we were on the Royal Mile in Edinburgh watching groups of Leinster and Munster supporters kicking balls up and down the road. Then the scale of the Leinster support really hit home when we got to the ground. It was incredible.'

ROCKY ELSOM: 'The one thing that I noticed on the way to the ground was the sheer volume of supporters in the city. Something that we were all conscious of was the expense of travelling and we had all heard stories about the great lengths the Leinster supporters had made to get there. As we pulled into the ground there was that giant banner image of me again! I allowed myself a wry smile this time.'

GORDON D'ARCY: 'Every hour in the build-up to the final seemed longer than the previous. The last 14 hours were absolute torture.'

SIMON KEOGH: 'That coach journey to the ground was the closest I've ever felt to being involved in an international game. The supporters coming out on to the streets to welcome us made the hair on the back of your neck stand up.'

JONATHAN SEXTON: 'Once the warm-up finished and the game got under way I was quite calm, and I suppose I needed to be. The drop goal was instinctive. It was in my head from seeing someone do it in the warm-up. I always enjoyed having a go since my schooldays so I just gave it a lash and thankfully I struck it well.

'You can have good days when they come off or bad days, like in Croke

ABOVE: Cian Healy lowers his head in preparation for the collision

Park a few weeks back, when I had two shocking efforts! Before that game I must have kicked twenty drop goals every day for the three weeks before the game and then I did barely any before the final and I hit one like that!

'The half-time break was good. I said a few words. I think that out-halves should feel comfortable talking in a group setting because you are one of the main decision-makers and need to organize the team. I have also captained sides right the way up so it wasn't that big a deal. It was something along the lines of us having to score first in the second half and that it was written for us to win this game because of all the hardships we had come through together. I then got a bit worried because I didn't want some people's heads dropping if we didn't score first so I kind of had to backtrack a bit!'

TREVOR HOGAN: 'It was fairly tough not being in the squad for the final, to be honest, because I travelled with the team the day before and did everything with the lads, including the warm-up. But then you just have to put your

gear back on as the game kicks off and leave it up to the lads on the pitch. It's hard, but if you have your head down and go into a decline you're no use to anybody. We had real strength in unity this year and that helped us.

'The attitude that best exemplifies the team ethos for me was summed up by Felipe in the semi-final. After his injury against Munster I sat beside him in the dugout and he was on such a high, feeding off the excitement of the occasion, celebrating the high of victory and cheering Sexto's performance, despite his own serious injury. It was almost surreal to see him hopping around on his crutches in delight! It highlighted the sense of unity that was in all of us this year and that drove the squad on even when we had our own setbacks.'

BERNARD JACKMAN: 'The words "next ball" had become a bit of a catchphrase for us all year. It basically meant don't dwell on mistakes. I remember Jamie dropping the ball with five minutes to go and Johnny Sexton was shouting and you could see this look of calmness on Jamie as he simply said, "Relax." Calm heads got us through those tense final moments.'

FELIPE CONTEPOMI: 'On the pitch you have control, but when you're not playing the tension is unbearable. After that game I understood what my wife means when she says that she has three heart attacks during every game! The 80 minutes felt like three days, while the last five minutes were eternal.

'Murrayfield has given us a few headaches over the years, but the final was a perfect game – the energy of the younger players combined with the hunger of the experienced players, which all came together at the right time.

❝ On the pitch you have control, but when you're not playing the tension is unbearable. After that game I understood what my wife means when she says that she has three heart attacks during every game! **❞**

LEFT: Shane Horgan dances past Julien Dupuy on the touchline

'When the final whistle went I forgot my recuperation and rushed to the field. Probably the only anxious moment that I had in the aftermath was when I was carried aloft with the trophy by some of the non-playing 22, because they seemed to have been on the beer …'

SHANE JENNINGS: 'I was at the bottom of a ruck when all I could see was the referee's hand up to award us a penalty. I remember Mal shouting, "That's it, we've won."'

ISA NACEWA: 'It was the sight of [reserve scrum-half] Paul O'Donohoe running on to the field that told me we had won. I was standing at the back because they were in possession and any lapse in concentration could have cost us the game at that stage. My parents back home were over the moon. Around twelve of my friends had stayed up half the night with their wives and partners to watch the game and the next morning messages started flooding in from friends and family back in Auckland and it really hit home.'

NEXT PAGE: Leo Cullen and Chris Whitaker – captain and vice-captain – await the presentation of medals and trophy

LEFT: Rocky Elsom takes a high ball with support from Shane Jennings

ABOVE: Stan Wright and Bernard Jackman find they enjoy the feel of silverware

ROCKY ELSOM: 'On the final whistle I remember hugging Shane Horgan. The winning feeling for me was immediate because all of the non-playing 22 ran on to the field. It was just incredible. There was such a connection with the crowd at that time because we had all come through the same journey together.'

JOHN FOGARTY: 'The reality of the win sunk in with me when I was shaving after the game. It was the first time I looked in the mirror and amidst all the happiness and excitement all I could think about was family. My dad popped into my head and I'm sure he would have been a very proud man. I had uncles, aunts, cousins and friends over from Ireland as well as my sister and mum, who had to put up with Stephen Keogh before the game! Having them there meant so much to me.

'I thought about my daughter Katie May and my wife Sinéad, who has followed me from Cork to Galway and now to Dublin, involving seven or eight moves, which must have been so unsettling for her, but she has made

things so easy for me and I love her for that. You just can't thank those you love enough for all that they do for you. My mum and Sinéad have sacrificed so much for me to get there and that trophy was a small reward for their faith and support over the years.'

ABOVE: Rocky Elsom, Brian O'Driscoll, the injured Felipe Contepomi and Gordon D'Arcy

SHANE JENNINGS: 'The week before the final I was assigned media duty for the Sunday papers previewing the final and there was talk of Geordy's [Leicester captain Geordan Murphy] comments about Leinster being a Dublin club. I think he was just trying to stir a pot to see if we'd take the bait. We had a drink in the dressing-room after the game, and you could see from the reception he got as he came off the high regard that both sets of supporters held him in.'

LEO CULLEN: 'In the aftermath of the game I hardly got a minute to myself to allow the win to sink in. I was being pulled all over the place with round after round of interviews, as well as stitches to a head wound. But one of

ABOVE: Brian O'Driscoll with his fiancée, the actress and novelist Amy Huberman

the highlights was seeing my dad on the pitch and it was a nice memory to get in a photo with him. I spoke to a few of the Tigers players and they were pretty happy with their season. They seemed to see the bigger picture in the context of their season overall and how far they'd come after being in disarray earlier in the campaign.'

BRIAN O'DRISCOLL: 'A couple of years back I had seriously thought about pursuing a new challenge in a new country, but it meant so much for me to win with a group of players, many of whom I've grown up with. There were die-hard Leinster men who we had the backing of at home and at the game, which is why I mentioned some of the players in the post-match interviews. Guys like Victor [Costello], Reggie [Corrigan], Denis [Hickie] and Gleeso [Keith Gleeson] deserved to share in the euphoria and I would have loved for them to be on the pitch sharing in the moment with us. We walked around the ground and it was great to share the joy with friends and family, including my two little nieces Katie and Aoife. It felt

so sweet to win this trophy with the team I love.'

ABOVE: Shane Horgan enjoys a moment alone with the trophy

SHANE HORGAN: 'Relief and elation. They were the foremost emotions for me in the dressing-room after the game. There are so many people who have helped Leinster reach this stage, who have helped shape the culture of the team and were part of the sea-change going back over years. I would have loved for each of them to be a part of the win. I'm sure that they shared our delight.'

STEPHEN KEOGH: 'At the end of the match there was just a feeling of happiness for the fans, who were magnificent all day, and the players, who had strived for years to win the trophy, as well as those who were leaving. For the non-playing members it was hard to enjoy the game because you put so much effort into the year and it all came down to the last 80 minutes. Eighty minutes to define your season. I know from experience with Munster that the first European title is the hardest one to win.'

CHAPTER SIXTEEN

REGGIE CORRIGAN: 'When I first started playing professional rugby a European title was a pipe dream. Yes, we could win one-off matches against the bigger teams, but as a team and as an organization it seemed as though we were light years away from the consistency of the likes of Leicester, Bath or Toulouse. I know how hard everybody behind the scenes has worked at Leinster over the years to get us to this point and that this hasn't just happened by accident.

'We can now realistically think about maintaining our place in Europe and maybe with Ireland pushing on and winning a World Cup, both of which were unheard of before. Winning the Heineken Cup, on the back of the Grand Slam, has enabled supporters of all ages to dream.'

MICHAEL CHEIKA: 'My highlight from the final was the moment of real, genuine happiness at the final whistle. It's rare you get that kind of emotion in life any more.

'Since day one we have tried to build a winning culture and set standards

ABOVE: The backroom boys: Garreth Farrell, Chris Dennis, Emmet Farrell, Jason Cowman, James Allen, Stephen Smith, Mike Thompson

of excellence in everything we do to make Leinster a team that the supporters, players staff and everyone else can be proud of. This was our final stamp on asserting that culture.'

CHRIS WHITAKER: 'It was a bizarre feeling after the final whistle. I didn't want to jump around and show emotion because I always felt that we could win it. I saw Leo talking to some of the guys before the presentation and it was then that he told me that we were going to receive the trophy together. I was embarrassed because, firstly, I'm not Irish. Secondly, I felt that there were other players who were more worthy to be up there.

'To be honest, the only thing I was concerned about at that stage was that some of the non-playing 22 weren't going to receive a medal. Players like Gary Brown, Chris Keane, Trevor Hogan and Stephen Keogh, to name but a few, had contributed hugely all season but were unfortunate to miss out on the final squad. I will always have my memories from playing that day, but they deserved some recognition. You could see how much it meant to them because they were the first people to run on to the pitch in victory.'

LEO CULLEN: 'Whits has been an integral part of the team over the last few years and, in my eyes, it was only right that he share the stage with me at the presentation because he had captained the team on many occasions over the course of the season. The team has great respect for him. As well as being a great servant he's humble, a great man to be around the dressing-room and someone who has been a big help to me personally. It was only right he shared the moment. Typical Whits, it did take a bit of persuading with him …'

Leicester 16, Leinster 19
Saturday, 23 May 2009

Murrayfield, 5 p.m.
Attendance: 66,523

LEICESTER: 15: Geordan Murphy, captain (Matt Smith, 47), 14: Scott Hamilton, 13: Ayoola Erinle, 12: Dan Hipkiss, 11: Alesana Tuilagi, 10: Sam Vesty, 9: Julien Dupuy (Harry Ellis, 75); 1: Marcos Ayerza, 2: George Chuter (Benjamin Kayser, 55), 3: Martin Castrogiovanni (Julian White, 52), 4: Tom Croft, 5: Ben Kay, 6: Craig Newby, 7: Ben Woods (Lewis Moody, 60), 8: Jordan Crane (Louis Deacon, 29)

LEINSTER: 15: Isa Nacewa, 14: Shane Horgan, 13: Brian O'Driscoll, 12: Gordon D'Arcy, 11: Luke Fitzgerald (Rob Kearney, 71), 10: Jonathan Sexton, 9: Chris Whitaker; 1: Cian Healy (Ronan McCormack, 60–64), 2: Bernard Jackman (John Fogarty, 55), 3: Stan Wright, 4: Leo Cullen, captain, 5: Malcolm O'Kelly, 6: Rocky Elsom. 7: Shane Jennings (Ronan McCormack, 35–42), 8: Jamie Heaslip

REPLACEMENTS NOT USED: Devin Toner, Sean O'Brien, Simon Keogh, Girvan Dempsey

LEICESTER SCORERS: B. Woods (1 try), J. Dupuy (3 penalties, 1 conversion)

LEINSTER SCORERS: J. Heaslip (1 try), J. Sexton (2 penalties, 1 drop goal, 1 conversion), B. O'Driscoll (1 drop goal)

REFEREE: Nigel Owens (Wales)

CHAPTER 17
THE GAME OF THE FATHER

❝ For every legacy there is a beginning, for every dream a simple observation. ❞

Parenthood is a hell of a ride. It starts the moment your child is born, and never really lets up in intensity. The good times are great; you get to share in all the joy. But there are disappointments too and that's when you have to be strong.

Every journey has a starting point. This one, appropriately enough, started with a whistle. Half-time in the 1988 Millennium match between Ireland and England, and as the players thundered off the Lansdowne Road turf, the Under-10s of Willow Park and Terenure ran on to the pitch for an exhibition match.

Under bright blue skies – it was an unseasonably warm April afternoon – the schoolboys played out their match of cheerful chaos, little knowing that Lansdowne Road would become a second home to some of them. And when the final whistle went, a tall blond boy named Cullen, L., raised his arms in triumph.

The children left their hallowed turf that day, emotionally spent but visibly beaming. For Frank Cullen, in a small pocket of Lansdowne Road on that spring day in 1988, the dream began.

'I'll never forget that day. All the Willow lads were beaming as they came

LEFT: Leo Cullen with his father, Frank, after the Heineken Cup final

off the pitch but nobody in the stadium had a bigger smile than me. Just
to see Leo playing on that pitch and being as happy as only a ten-year-old
can be … it was one of life's magical moments, my heart was bursting
with pride.

'The Heineken Cup final was a thousand highlights all rolled into one
day. There were so many moments that I'll remember forever. Like at the
end of the match, I was trying to get on to the pitch but the ERC officials
wouldn't let me – it was like Fort Knox. Then someone (who will remain
nameless!) threw me their accreditation and I was able to get on and
share the celebrations on the pitch.

'The hug I received from Leo (who later gave me his medal) and then
Malcolm was something to be experienced. The adrenalin coming off the
lads was electrifying. I was so proud to be there, watching the presentation
and the lap of honour in front of a sea of blue flags and jerseys, just being
in a special place at an incredibly special time. It was like reaching a
mountaintop.

'I thought that once the trophy was presented, nothing would separate Leo from it. But if you look at the footage, the first thing he did was hand it on to someone else. That's Leo. He was basically saying the triumph was not about him but the team. It was the same when he insisted that the entire squad – even those who weren't in the 22 on the day – go up for the presentation, and the same when he made Chris [Whitaker] accept the trophy with him.

'That brought me back to the incredible gesture that Leicester Tigers made a couple of years previously when they invited two foreign players in Leo and Shane Jennings – who they knew were leaving at the end of the season – up to accept the Premiership trophy. I know how much of an indelible mark that made on the two boys.

'Leicester Tigers Chairman Peter Tom and Cockers [Richard Cockerill] were very gracious in defeat and were genuinely pleased for us despite their disappointment. It just brought home to me again what a magnificent club Leicester is, with exceptional community values and humility. I had a quiet word with Cockers and thanked him for all he had done for Leo, and as he was walking away something must have struck a chord because he turned back and gave me a wry smile.

'The scenes in Edinburgh Airport were unforgettable. I wouldn't say there was a drop left in any of the beer taps by the time the flights started leaving! When Paula and I boarded our plane the pilot welcomed the parents of the winning captain and we got a lovely reception, but Paula still hadn't spoken to Leo amidst all the chaos at the ground and in the airport, so she was peppering to get home.

'We landed in Dublin a little ahead of the team, and our timing was perfect – just as we arrived at the gate Leo walked through the next gate

" I thought that once the trophy was presented, nothing would separate Leo from it. But if you look at the footage, the first thing he did was hand it on to someone else. That's Leo. "

with the trophy and that was the first opportunity he had to meet his mother. More hugs and joyous moments.

'From there it was off to the Burlington for a reception for the players, management, branch officials and friends and families who had travelled back from Edinburgh. It was really only then that the magnitude of the day started to sink in. I remember sitting at a table at 1 a.m. with Leo, Paula and the trophy… and to be able to say that Leinster was the home of the European champions was an incredible feeling.

'And to have done it the hard way made it all the more enjoyable – beating former champions Wasps, coming through an epic encounter with Harlequins, an even more epic battle against the reigning champions Munster (surely the sweetest of all victories for Leinster fans), and of course glory in the final against the most successful Heineken Cup team of all and Leo's former club – Leicester Tigers. It couldn't have been planned any better.

'On the Tuesday evening after the final Leo brought the cup back to our family home near Newtownmountkennedy. We invited a few family friends and neighbouring farmers and a huge crowd turned up. We had people coming up saying things like "I was down in the Poor Clares saying a prayer for you," while others were on to St Anthony. Every little helped! I was astonished at the excitement and passion of people whom I would not have expected to have been so interested in rugby.

'This victory touched every town and village across the province. People love to identify with localized success or local sporting heroes and it comes back to the strong GAA ethos of having pride in your community and supporting your local team. It was a time for everybody to share in the joy of finally conquering Europe.'

HOMECOMING

" Imagine getting on this plane having lost the game… **"**

Preparations went on behind the scenes that week to prepare a homecoming in the RDS in the event of the squad winning the trophy. Stage-builders travelled through the night to erect scaffolding and thousands turned up to acknowledge the returning heroes.

Over 120,000 commemorative posters were printed and distributed in the *Irish Times* that Monday, with notes of congratulations coming in from schools, clubs and well-wishers from all walks of life.

CHRIS WHITAKER: 'My father and mum originally come from Sevenoaks in Kent, and are '£10 Poms' – part of the generation of English people who left to live and work in Australia as part of a recruitment drive by the Australian government after the Second World War. So I suppose you could safely say that the love of adventure and travelling are embedded in me from them. Straight after the game I'd usually be straight on to my family back home who would have stayed up to watch games.

'Reading and replying to text messages nearly becomes part of your post-match routine and it's always touching to hear from home. It meant the world to me that dad was there in Edinburgh. But as we boarded the

ABOVE: Chris Whitaker makes his way through Dublin Airport with two of his daughters

flight that night, taking into account the reception we'd just received in the airport, the thought that kept running through my mind was, "Imagine getting on this plane having lost the game …"'

JOHN FOGARTY: 'I got some stick for the homecoming. There were pictures of Leo and me holding the trophy but Cheiks had it up on stage and he gave it to the first person he saw. Nobody would take it off me so that's how a young fella from Tipp wound up on the front page of the morning papers with the trophy!'

GIRVAN DEMPSEY: 'You can get wrapped up in your own performance and in yourself at times, but visiting Crumlin and Temple Street Children's hospitals after the final brought it home for all of us. You talk to the staff, the families and the patients themselves and see the hardships that they go through every day and you feel so privileged to be able to do what we do for a living.

'I'm going to become a father this year for the first time and all you want for your child is for him or her to be happy and healthy. Looking into the patients' eyes and speaking to them even for a short time left me with an impression of sadness, yes, at the obstacles they're facing at such a young age, but it also fills you with hope. I suppose it just puts everything in perspective.'

BRIAN O'DRISCOLL: 'There was a real feeling of satisfaction that we had finally managed it. The celebrations were short-lived for those of us who were travelling to South Africa with the Lions because we were due to catch the early-morning flight to London, so I had gone home to bed by the time Denis [Hickie] came into the party that night in the Krystle nightclub, which was a shame because we were all a bit disappointed not to share in the success with the team. But the Lions tour was as good a reason as any not to be too downhearted!'

ABOVE: Girvan Dempsey, Shane Horgan, Leo Cullen and Sean O'Brien visiting a young patient in Crumlin Children's Hospital

> ❝ There's a batch of young players in Leinster and Ireland who have only known success and there's a real humility and appreciation that years like this don't come around too often. ❞

ROB KEARNEY: 'When the final whistle sounded, the enormity of the situation just hit you. Hundreds of Leinster players had tried their hardest to bring the province to the promised land and for whatever reasons it just didn't happen for them.

'There were great celebrations going on back home and there's a part of me that would have loved to have been able to soak in the atmosphere, but at the same time I knew how privileged I was to be going to South Africa. It was only in the days afterwards when the win began to hit home. There's a batch of young players in Leinster and Ireland who have only known success and there's a real humility and appreciation that years like this don't come around too often. It has been an incredible year and one that will live long in the memory.'

KURT MCQUILKIN: 'On the Sunday night after the game the coaching staff went to Kiely's pub in Donnybrook to mark the win, and it's the little things you remember. Looking around that pub that night it reminded me of the generations of past Leinster players who had toasted success and consoled themselves after defeats there.

'The owner, Pat Cremin, and the bar staff had been there with us along the journey, always offering a consoling arm around the shoulder and never judging. Coming from New Zealand, I never felt that Leinster "D4" thing that people sometimes referred to. All I know is that everybody had played a small part in this success.'

BERNARD JACKMAN: 'I've been coaching for the last few years with Newbridge, Tullow, and this year with Coolmine, and have been fortunate to work in three of the four communities, along with Clontarf, who helped me develop as a player, but more importantly as a man. Watching the commitment of amateurs training twice a week to compete for their friends and for the pride of their local community is a reminder of how lucky I was to have been one of the first crop of professional players in Ireland.

'When I think of the journey that has taken me to Manchester, Galway and now back home in Leinster I have to pinch myself. A few years back I put my career on hold for one last crack in the AIL with 'Tarf to try and earn a professional contract. I hoped that one day I might pull on the blue shirt of my home province. Dreams aren't supposed to come true.'

RONAN McCORMACK: 'I'm one of six brothers, all lifelong Leinster supporters, each of whom would have played at one stage with St Mary's College school and later for the club. It's fantastic for my family to see me playing with the team that we have all supported since our teenage years. The only thing that got me through those tough times at the turn of the year was my desire to pull on the blue jersey.'

JONATHAN SEXTON: 'There were interview requests coming in from four Sunday papers and radio stations the week after the final and it was strange. I felt that I had worked hard all year and all of a sudden my rewards came at once. It was weird, people recognizing you on the street, but it was nice. I remember going down to visit relatives in Listowel the following weekend and there were pictures of me in a Leinster jersey. I'm not sure how well that went down with the locals, but it meant a great deal to me.'

JOHN FOGARTY: 'There's a small cabinet back home in my mother's house. In it you'll find a number of keepsakes such as AIL medals, my brother Damian's football and hurling medals, Munster Schools Junior and Senior Cup medals courtesy of Denis, and an award for drama that I won a few years back, now gathering dust. How I got that one, you might ask, I'll never know! Tucked at the back of that cabinet was the silver memento from the 2002 final. As I stared at it I had subconsciously written myself out of ever having another opportunity to further myself at that same stage. My time had come and gone, or so it seemed. Now that silver ornament has a new golden friend to accompany it.'

SEAN O'BRIEN: 'There were a few of us selected for the Churchill Cup campaign ten days after the final, so the weekend before we headed off to the USA I took the trophy down to Tullow RFC, where the journey in rugby began for me. It was my way of saying thank you to a great club without whom I might never have played the game.'

GORDON D'ARCY: 'I started my twelfth season in professional rugby this year, so this win was a long time coming. The magnitude only sank in when I got home to Wexford at the end of the Lions tour. I went down to my favourite pub, amongst friends and family, and it all sank in. To finally get to this stage is an amazing feeling.'

SHANE JENNINGS: 'The weekend after the final I went down to Achill Island for a short break with friends via Ballymahon in Longford, where my mother Joan's family come from. I have fond memories of summers and long weekends in Longford growing up. My grandmother lived there for many years and I have aunts and cousins who are big supporters of Leinster, while my uncle Sean would come up for every game.

'It was great to see the joy, the photos of the team in Clarke's Pub on the Dublin Road and just the goodwill that was there for us. For me it just hit home that we're not a one-county team. Each of us has roots that we're proud of right across the country.'

GIRVAN DEMPSEY: 'A week after the final my wife and I were queuing up in Dublin Airport ahead of a short break to Portugal. Out of the corner of my eye I noticed a small group of schoolboys nudging and whispering. There seemed to be real sense of excitement in their faces so after our bags had gone through I posed for a few photos.

'As we made our way I said thanks to their mother, who was with them, for their support, to which she replied, "Thanks, Felipe, for all you've done for us over the years and the best of luck in Toulon!" As we passed through security I then met Bernard Jackman, who was also by coincidence on the flight, and he said to me, "This is weird. Apparently Felipe's on the flight too. Have you seen him?"'

LEFT: A week and a half after bidding Leinster fans a tearful farewell at the RDS, Felipe Contepomi is all smiles as he greets supporters at the same ground

> **❝** The difference with a final is that the accomplishment will last through time. That medal is a recognition which you can be truly proud of and I'm just glad that it happened with Leinster. **❞**

STAN WRIGHT: 'I went back to Auckland after the Heineken Cup final and spent a week in the Cook Islands. News of the Heineken Cup win was big back home. They even had my picture on the front page of the main Saturday paper, *The Cook Island News*, which was a big deal. There was great interest in the quarters, semis and final, which were all shown live. We're a small nation, but we're proud of our own. It was nice.'

MALCOLM O'KELLY: 'Experience is a funny thing. An interesting bit of advice I once received was that if you win a match or lose a match, irrespective, the result is forgotten in 24 hours. It's a very negative outlook, but I think it's meant as a way of dealing with defeat more than anything. The difference with a final is that the accomplishment will last through time. That medal is a recognition which you can be truly proud of and I'm just glad that it happened with Leinster.'

LEO CULLEN: 'There's an element of sacrifice involved in supporting teams and as a group one of our deep-rooted motivations over the course of the last few years has been to give 100 per cent every game to honour all those who turn up to support us.

'We scrapped for everything all season and you could even see in our last home game of the season against the Scarlets, six days after the semi-final, that the commitment was there and it was our duty to go out and put in a performance of real substance. I believe that that work ethic ultimately drove us over the line.'

ACKNOWLEDGEMENTS

This book would not have been possible without the co-operation of the following people.

To Michael McLoughlin, Brendan Barrington and all the team in Penguin, sincere thanks for your guidance and support over the course of this project. If the saying is true that every picture tells a thousand words, then to Billy Stickland and his team in Inpho Photography, it was your vision that inspired each tale. The author would also like to thank Reggie Corrigan, Victor Costello, Frank Cullen, Denis Hickie and Stephanie O'Kelly. Special thanks also to the ever-inventive David Cahill for his designs and to all the Leinster supporters who played their part in this journey. To all my colleagues in Leinster Rugby, particularly Mick Dawson and Keira Kennedy, thank you for your co-operation and assistance. To all the players and coaches who inspired the words from Denver to Sydney, via Cape Town and Thailand, there was no request too large, too late or too peculiar that you would not assist with. On behalf of the many lives you have enhanced in different ways, I hope that I have done some justice to your remarkable deeds. Finally, to my family and friends, especially Nikki, my parents John and Colette, and my brothers Kenneth, Mark, David and Alan, thank you for your love and support.

PETER BREEN

PHOTO CREDITS